PENGUIN BOOKS

THE THING ABOUT LIFE IS THAT ONE DAY YOU'LL BE DEAD

'Enthralling . . . Fascinating . . . Ultimately, the humanity of Shields's interior and exterior exploration is what makes *The Thing About Life* – and life itself – worthwhile' *San Francisco Chronicle*

'An edifying, unclassifiable mixture of filial love and Oedipal rage' *Time*

'A primer on ageing and death for those who take theirs without the sugar . . . There's a comfort to be found in this sober investigation of morality, in Shields's clear-eyed look at the ways in which we come undone' *Esquire*

'The book is self-obsessed in the best sense, obsessed with the wonder of being here, moment to moment. Reading it, one feels oneself dying and so is reminded of just how alive we are' Matt Weiland

'Breathtaking . . . Shields had us laughing out loud, even in the face of death' *Time Out* Chicago

'Mr Shields is a sharp-eyed, self-deprecating, at times hilarious writer. Approaching the flat line of the last page, we want more' *Wall Street Journal*

'A joyous, thrilling, and funny riff on life and the human body. Shields has written a love letter to life, while talking quite a bit about how our bodies march us straight toward death' *Seattle Times*

'Many writers aim to capture the human condition in all its variety, audacity, and ⟨...⟩ ⟨...⟩ ⟨...⟩ close to their targ⟨...⟩ ⟨...⟩ rest of artistic acc⟨...⟩ ⟨...⟩ruition'

'Shields undergoes his midlife crisis and comes out the other side – more accessible than ever before, more tender, "nicer". And yet *The Thing About Life* adroitly sidesteps sentimentality – very hard to do when the core of it is a son's love for his cranky, tenacious, irascible, geriatric, Jewish father. I love this book' David Guterson

'A darting and even breezy read, rigorous when it needs to be but also wry and dryly tender . . . Shields's prose has an easy gait, but he gets at something hard and thorny' *Salon*

'A true inspiration . . . *The Thing About Life* is at times both poignant and profound without trying too hard to be either. It is a book that everyone – young and old – should read and appreciate, for it gives us all deeper insights into the curiosities and minutiae of life' *Anniston Star*

'Oddly cheery . . . A darkly funny examination of the least funny thing' *Toronto Star*

'Full of happy surprises . . . This odd study of life and death is as funny and informal as it is instructive and life-affirming . . . So deftly interwoven are the factual and the personal throughout that Shields seems to have created a whole new genre' *Providence Journal*

'It's a bold writer who dares to tackle head-on the subject of what it means to be human – something that David Shields does with an extraordinary mixture of tenderness, humour, and inexhaustible curiosity' Jonathan Raban

'Shields is after bigger literary game: his books are to be taken as exemplars of a new literature that has slowly been gearing up to knock fiction off its complacently dominant perch' *Hartford Courant*

'Invigorating, filled with page-turning stories, laugh-out-loud moments, and breathtaking revelations. At the end, as in life, you are left wondering: is it really already over? Can't I have more? I absolutely love this book' Pauline Chen

'Intriguing . . . [A] radically thought-provoking reflection on the nature of our bodies and whatever kind of meaning we can assign to them while the heart is still pumping and the neurons are still firing' *Rocky Mountain News*

The Thing About Life
Is That
One Day
You'll Be Dead

DAVID SHIELDS

PENGUIN BOOKS

PENGUIN BOOKS

Published by the Penguin Group
Penguin Books Ltd, 80 Strand, London WC2R ORL, England
Penguin Group (USA), Inc., 375 Hudson Street, New York, New York 10014, USA
Penguin Group (Canada), 90 Eglinton Avenue East, Suite 700, Toronto, Ontario, Canada M4P 2Y3
(a division of Pearson Penguin Canada Inc.)
Penguin Ireland, 25 St Stephen's Green, Dublin 2, Ireland (a division of Penguin Books Ltd)
Penguin Group (Australia), 250 Camberwell Road, Camberwell, Victoria 3124, Australia
(a division of Pearson Australia Group Pty Ltd)
Penguin Books India Pvt Ltd, 11 Community Centre, Panchsheel Park, New Delhi – 110 017, India
Penguin Group (NZ), 67 Apollo Drive, Rosedale, Auckland 0632, New Zealand
(a division of Pearson New Zealand Ltd)
Penguin Books (South Africa) (Pty) Ltd, 24 Sturdee Avenue, Rosebank,
Johannesburg 2196, South Africa

Penguin Books Ltd, Registered Offices: 80 Strand, London WC2R ORL, England

www.penguin.com

First published in the United States of America
by Alfred A. Knopf, a division of Random House, Inc., New York 2008
First published in Great Britain by Penguin Books 2010
This edition published in Penguin Books 2011

1

My deep gratitude to the John Simon Guggenheim Foundation, Artist Trust, and the
Simpson Center for the Humanities for fellowships that enabled me to complete this book.

Printed in Great Britain by Clays Ltd, St Ives plc

A CIP catalogue record for this book is available from the British Library

ISBN: 978-0-141-04949-6

www.greenpenguin.co.uk

Penguin Books is committed to a sustainable future
for our business, our readers and our planet.
The book in your hands is made from paper
certified by the Forest Stewardship Council.

For my father, 1910–

CONTENTS

Adolescence

Adulthood and Middle Age

Old Age and Death

That, finally, is all it means to be alive:
to be able to die.

—J. M. Coetzee

The Thing About Life Is That
One Day You'll Be Dead

PROLOGUE

Letter to My Father

Let the wrestling match begin: my stories versus his stories.

This book is an autobiography of my body, a biography of my father's body, an anatomy of our bodies together—especially my dad's, his body, his relentless body.

This is my research; this is what I now know: the brute facts of existence, the fragility and ephemerality of life in its naked corporeality, human beings as bare, forked animals, the beauty and pathos in my body and his body and everybody else's body as well.

Accept death, I always seem to be saying.

Accept life, is his entirely understandable reply.

Why am I half in love with easeful death? I just turned 51. As Martin Amis has said, "Who knows when it happens, but it happens. Suddenly you realize that you're switching from saying 'Hi' to saying 'Bye.' And it's a full-time job: death. You really have to wrench your head around to look in the other direction, because death's so apparent now, and it wasn't apparent before. You were intellectually persuaded that you were going to die, but it wasn't a reality." So, too, for myself, being the father of an annoyingly vital 14-year-old girl only deepens these feelings. I'm no longer athletic (really bad back—more on this later). Natalie is. After a soccer game this season, a parent of one of the players on the other team came up to her and said, "Turn pro."

Why, at 97, is my father so devoted to longevity per se, to sheer survival? He is—to me—cussedly, maddeningly alive and interesting, but I also don't want to romanticize him. He's life force as life machine—exhausting and exhaustive. Rest in peace? Hard to imagine.

Mark Harris, trying to explain why he thought Saul Bellow was a better writer than any of his contemporaries, said Bellow was simply more alive than anyone else, and there's something of that in my father. D. H. Lawrence was said to have lived as if he were a man without skin. That, too, is my father: I keep on urging him to don skin, and he keeps declining.

I seem to have an Oedipal urge to bury him in a shower of death data. Why do I want to cover my dad in an early shroud? He's strong and he's weak and I love him and I hate him and I want him to live forever and I want him to die tomorrow.

Infancy and Childhood

Our Birth Is Nothing
but Our Death Begun

A fetus doesn't sit passively in its mother's womb and wait to be fed. Its placenta aggressively sprouts blood vessels that invade its mother's tissues to extract nutrients. A mother and her unborn child engage in an unconscious struggle over the nutrients she will provide it. Pregnancy is, as the evolutionary biologist David Haig says, a tug of war: each side pulls hard; the flag tied to the middle of the rope barely moves. Existence is warfare.

Human beings have existed for 250,000 years; during that time, 90 billion individuals have lived and died. You're one of 6.5 billion people now on the planet, and 99.9 percent of your genes are the same as everyone else's. The difference is in the remaining 0.1 percent—one nucleotide base in every 1,000.

You're born with 350 bones (long, short, flat, and irregular); as you grow, the bones fuse together: an adult's body has 206 bones. Approximately 70 percent of your body weight is water—which is about the same percentage of the earth's surface that is water.

A newborn baby, whose average heart rate is 120 beats per minute, makes the transition from a comfortable, fluid-filled environment to a cold, air-filled one by creating a suction 50

times stronger than the average adult breath. I was a breech
birth, the danger of which is that the head (in this case, my
head) comes out last, which dramatically increases the possibility that the umbilical cord will get wrapped around the neck
(in this case, my neck). I entered the world feet first, then
remained in the hospital an extra week to get a little R & R in a
warm incubator that my father guarded like a goalie whenever
anyone came within striking distance. If I lay still for more
than a few minutes, my father reportedly pounded on the glass
dome. I wasn't dead, Dad. I was only sleeping. All my life I've
pretended to seek a cold, air-filled environment (danger), but
really what I'm drawn to is that comfortable, fluid-filled environment (safety).

I remember once being complimented by my mother for
not entering a playground when the gate was locked and my
father being disgusted that I hadn't climbed the fence. As a
wide receiver, I would run intricate patterns, then stand all
alone in the middle of the field, waving my hands, calling for
the ball. I never dropped a pass, but when I was hit hard, I
would typically tighten up and fumble. I was the best softball
player in the neighborhood, but as we grew older, we began to
play overhand, fast-pitch hardball, and I started flinching. Trying to beat out a ground ball, I would always slow down so that
the throw to first base would arrive ahead of me and I'd avoid
getting hit in the head with a wild toss. Batting, I was afraid of
getting hit with the pitch; fielding, I dreaded bad hops off the
rocky infield. I could run 100 yards in 10.8 seconds, but I had
very long legs and the track coach insisted that I run high
hurdles; I stutter-stepped before each hurdle to make sure I
cleared it and came in last. Having never learned to dive, I
jumped in the pool feet first. The swimming instructor
dragged me to the edge of the diving board, positioned my

arms and legs, held me in the air for a second, then dropped me into the pool. At the last instant, I turned my face, and water broke my fall like a bed of electric needles. What was I scared of? Why have I always been so afraid of getting hurt?

In the *Bhagavad Gītā*, the human body is defined as a wound with nine openings.

A newborn baby is, objectively, no beauty. The fat pads that will fill out the cheeks are missing. The jaws are unsupported by teeth. Hair, if there is any, is often so fine as to make the baby (especially Caucasian babies) appear bald. Cheesy material—called vernix caseosa—covers the body, providing a protective dressing for the skin, which is reddened, moist, and deeply creased. Swelling formed by pressure during the passage through the birth canal may have temporarily deformed the nose, caused one or both eyes to swell up, or elongated the head into a strange shape. The skull is incompletely formed: in some places, the bones haven't fully joined together, leaving the brain covered only by soft tissue. External genitalia in both sexes are disproportionately larger because of stimulation by the mother's hormones. For the same reason, the baby's breasts may be somewhat enlarged and secrete a watery discharge called "witch's milk." The irises are pale blue; true eye color develops later. The head is very large in proportion to the body, and the neck can't support it, while the buttocks are tiny.

The average baby weighs 7¼ pounds and is 21 inches long. Newborns lose 5 to 8 percent of their birth weight in the first few days of life—owing, mainly, to water loss. They can hear little during the first 24 hours until air enters the eustachian tubes. They miss the womb and resent any stimulus. They will suck anything placed in or near their mouth. Their eyes wander and cross. Their body temperature is erratic, and their breathing is often irregular.

At 1 month, a baby can wobble its head and practice flexing its arms and legs. At 2 months, it can face straight ahead while lying on its back. On its stomach, it can lift its head about 45 degrees. At 3 months, a baby's neck muscles are strong enough to support its head for a second or two.

Babies are born with brains 25 percent of adult size, because the mechanics of walking upright impose a constraint on the size of the mother's pelvis; the channel through which the baby is born can't get any bigger. The baby's brain quickly makes up for that initial constraint: by age 1, the brain is 75 percent of adult size.

Infants have accurate hearing up to 40,000 cycles per second and may wince at a dog whistle that adults, who can't register sounds above 20,000 cycles per second, don't even notice. Your ears contain sensory hair cells, which turn mechanical fluid energy inside the cochlea into electrical signals that can be picked up by nerve cells; these electrical signals are delivered to the brain and allow you to hear. Beginning at puberty, these hair cells begin to disappear, decreasing your ability to hear specific frequencies; higher tones are the first to go.

A newborn's hands tend to be held closed, but if the area between the thumb and forefinger is stroked, the hand clenches it and holds on with sufficient strength to support the baby's weight if both hands are grasping. This innate "grasp reflex" serves no purpose in the human infant but was crucial in the last prehuman phase of evolution when the infant had to cling to its mother's hair.

My father reminds me that according to Midrash—the ever-evolving commentary upon the Hebrew scriptures— when you arrive in the world as a baby, your hands are clenched, as though to say, "Everything is mine. I will inherit it all." When you depart from the world, your hands are open, as though to say, "I have acquired nothing from the world."

If a baby is dropped, an immediate change from the usual curled posture occurs, as all four extremities are flung out in extension. The "startle reflex," or "embrace reflex," probably once served to help a simian mother catch a falling infant by causing it to spread out as fully as possible.

When Natalie was born, I cried, and my wife, Laurie, didn't—too busy. One minute, we were in the hospital room, holding hands and reading magazines, and the next, Laurie looked at me, with a commanding seriousness I'd never seen in her before, and said, "Put down the magazine." Natalie emerged, smacking her lips, and I asked the nurse to reassure me that this didn't indicate diabetes (I'd been reading too many parent-to-be manuals). I vowed I would never again think a trivial or stupid or selfish thought; this exalted state didn't last, but still . . .

The Kogi Indians believe that when an infant begins life, it knows only three things: mother, night, and water.

Francis Thompson wrote, "For we are born in other's pain, / And perish in our own." Edward Young wrote, "Our birth is nothing but our death begun." Francis Bacon: "What then remains, but that we still should cry / Not to be born, or being born, to die?" The first sentence of Vladimir Nabokov's *Speak, Memory* is: "The cradle rocks above an abyss, and common sense tells us that our existence is but a brief crack of light between two eternities of darkness."

Much mentioned but rarely discussed: the tissue-thin separation between existence and non-. In 1919, at age 9, my father and his friends were crossing train tracks in Brooklyn when my father, last in line, stepped directly on the third rail, which transformed him from a happy vertical child into a horizontal conductor of electric current. The train came rattling down the tracks toward Milton Shildcrout, who, lying flat on his back, was powerless to prevent his own self-induced electrocution. (When I asked my father why he changed his name, he said that his WWII sergeant "had trouble reading words of more than two syllables printed in the daily camp bulletin; he also had trouble correctly pronouncing what he described as 'those god-awful New Yawk names.' He said, in his thick-as-molasses Southern accent, 'That name of yours, Corporal, is so danged long it wouldn't fit on a tombstone just in case ya step on one of Tojo's bullets when we go overseas. You should shorten it to something a grown man like me can pronounce. From now on, I'm going to call you Shieldsy.' A few weeks later, Sergeant Hill shortened it to Shields. And Shields it was for the 36 months I was assigned to the 164th Quartermaster Company. I got used to Shields and, when I returned from the war, had it changed.")

I wouldn't be here today, typing this sentence, if someone named Big Abe, a 17-year-old wrestler who wore black shirts and a purple hat, hadn't slid a long piece of dry wood between galvanized little Milt and the third rail, flipping him high into the air only seconds before the train passed. My father was bruised about the elbows and knees and, later in summer, was a near-corpse as flesh turned red, turned pink, turned black, and peeled away to lean white bone. Toenails and fingernails crumbled, and what few hairs he had on his body were shed until Miltie himself had nearly vanished. His father sued Long Island Rail Road for $100, which supposedly paid—no more, no less—for the doctor's visits once a week to check for infection.

Decline and Fall (i)

All mammals age; the only animals that don't age are some of the more primitive ones: sharks, alligators, Galapagos tortoises. There are different theories as to why humans age at the rate they do: aging is genetically controlled (maladapted individuals die out and well-adapted ones persevere); the rate of aging within each species has developed for the good of each species; an entropy-producing agent disrupts cells; smaller mammals tend to have high metabolic rates and die at an earlier age than larger mammals do; specific endocrine or immune systems are particularly vulnerable and accelerate dysfunction for the whole organism; errors in DNA transcription lead to genetic errors that accelerate death. All of these theories are disputed: no one knows why we age.

Schopenhauer said, "Just as we know our walking to be only a constantly prevented falling, so is the life of our body only a constantly prevented dying, an ever-deferred death." (Dad: "Why would a supposedly wise man want to think this way?")

"As we get older," the British poet Henry Reed helpfully observed, "we do not get any younger."

On average, infants sleep 20 hours a day, 1-year-olds sleep

9

13 hours a day, teenagers sleep 9 hours, 40-year-olds sleep 7 hours, 50-year-olds sleep 6 hours, and people 65 and older sleep 5 hours. As you get older, you spend more time lying awake at night and, once asleep, you're much more easily aroused. The production of melatonin, which regulates the sleep cycle, reduces with age—one of the reasons why older people experience more insomnia. By age 65, an unbroken night of sleep is rare; 20 percent of the night consists of lying awake. As I constantly have to remind my now light-sleeping father, people ages 73 to 92 awake, on average, 21 times a night owing to disordered breathing.

An infant breathes 40 to 60 times a minute; a 5-year-old, 24 to 26 times; an adolescent, 20 to 22 times; an adult (beginning at age 25), 16 times. Over the course of your life, you're likely to take about 850 million breaths.

As a mammal, you get "milk teeth" by the end of your first year, then a second set that emerges as you leave infancy. When children start school, most of them have all of their baby teeth, which they'll lose before they're 12. By 13, most children have acquired all of their permanent teeth except their wisdom teeth. The third molars, or "wisdom teeth," usually emerge between ages 20 and 21; their roots mature between ages 18 and 25. As you age, your plaque builds up, your gums retreat, your teeth wear down, and you have more cavities and periodontal disease. The last few years, as my father's gums have shrunk, bone has rubbed up against his dentures, causing pain whenever he chews.

Children's fingernails grow one millimeter a week. Toenails grow one-quarter as fast as fingernails—one millimeter a month. Pianists' and typists' fingernails grow faster than others'. Fingernail growth is fastest in November, slowest in

July, and less rapid at night. The first and fifth digits grow more slowly; in severe cold weather, fingernails grow more slowly. From age 30 until 80, fingernail growth slows by 50 percent. Contrary to myth, Dad, your nails and hair don't keep growing after you die.

Boys vs. Girls (i)

The XX and XY chromosome pairings create females and males, respectively. Females have an advantage in having two X chromosomes to rely on throughout life, because the second X chromosome provides a backup if something goes wrong with a gene on the first one. A female with a disease-carrying gene on one of her X chromosomes can use the normal gene on the other X chromosome and avoid the expression of the disease, though she still carries the gene.

Female is the "default" sex: if you don't get a signal to form testes, your germ cells form ovaries and you become female. It takes the positive action of genes on the Y chromosome to make a potentially female body into a male body.

Women have a slower metabolism than men, beginning at conception: male embryos divide faster than female ones. The faster metabolic rate makes men's cells more vulnerable to breakdown; the entire male life cycle is completed more promptly than the female one.

Y-bearing sperm travel a little faster than X-bearing sperm; about 51 percent of newborn babies are male. Even more than 51 percent of conceptions are male, but male fetuses are more likely to undergo spontaneous abortions, stillbirths, and miscarriages than females. Premature girls tend to fare better than premature boys do. More boys than girls die in infancy.

Despite their slower metabolism, girls, at birth, are more advanced in bone development than boys. By the time they start school, girls are ahead of boys by approximately one year, and by third grade they're one and a half years advanced.

Until I was 9, I was the fastest person I knew. I ran to the store, around the block, to school, up the stairs, away from people, with people, toward people, on dirt, on sand, on asphalt, on the beach, in bare feet, in sneakers, in sandals, in boots, in good thin tight shiny laced black shoes. I had no hair on my legs, had legs hard as rubber, tanned as an Indian. My girlfriend was 9 and ran, too. We ran together. We raced, and she won; I thought she got a false start and demanded a rematch. She said no. I took off my sneakers, threw them into the lake, stepped on twigs, rocks, glass in my bare feet. She ran away from me. A few years later she started smoking cigarettes, lost her wind, and became a cheerleader.

Origins

Holding on to the plastic strap that was attached to my rocking horse's ears and mouth (name: Peaches; it was peach-colored and I liked peaches), I hoisted myself onto the saddle and wriggled around in my pajamas until I was comfortable and ready to ride. One cracked glass eye shone out of the right side of his head, the left eye having shattered in a previous skirmish, and his mouth, once bright red and smiling, was now chipped away to a tight-lipped and unpainted pout. His nose, too, was bruised, with gashes for nostrils, and he had a thick brown mane that, extending from the crown of his head nearly to his waist, was made from my grandmother's discarded wigs and glued to the wood. I pulled on the plastic strap that served as the rein, wrapped it around my fist, and slid my feet into the leather stirrups that hung from his waist.

I bounced up and down and set him in motion, rocking, tilting, sliding. The runner skidded slightly on the wooden floor. I sat up, leaning forward, pressing my lips to the back of his hairy neck, and said, "Don't creak. Don't make noise." (Infantile, naïve, I thought I could talk to wooden animals.) I wrapped my arms around his neck and kicked my legs back and forth in the stirrups, then lay my cheek against the back of his

14

head, pressing myself to his curves and carved-out shapes. When he pitched forward, I scooted up toward the bottom of his spine, and when he swung back, I let go of the leather strap and leaned back as far as I could so that I was causing his motions at the same time I was trying to get in perfect rhythm with them. I twisted my hips and bounced my thighs until it felt warm under me. My pajamas itched and stuck to my legs. My skin felt wet. No one knew; no one could know. I knew it was private, but I didn't know why. Forgetting that I should have been in bed and, if not under the covers, at least not creating such a commotion, I rocked faster, drove him across the floor and toward the far wall by jerking my body forward in the seat and squeezing my knees into his sides.

When my father opened the door and turned on the light, I turned Peaches away from him and the runner glanced off his foot. It felt warm under me and I wasn't going to stop. "Giddyup."

"Daver Baver," my father said, clearly amused by my equestrianship but attempting to embody the law. Such is my memory, anyway; who knows how accurate these recollections are? I was 4, maybe 5. "Your mother and sister are trying to sleep. I was trying to sleep. You'll wake up the house."

"I'll be quiet, Daddy."

"You need to get back in bed, Daver B."

"But I'm not tired."

"Do you have any idea what time—"

"It feels so good."

Each time Peaches rocked forward, I bumped my crotch up against the smooth surface of the seat and my whole body tingled. I clutched my horse and made him lurch crazily away from my father and toward the wall. I bucked back and forth until it hurt and I couldn't ride any longer. My dad brought

Peaches to a halt from behind, picked me up by the waist, and twirled me round and round the room—Airplane!—then brought me down, tossing me onto the bed. Whee. Then he sang me to sleep with my favorite song, about a boy and his daddy and a mockingbird.

I have a recurring dream in which I open the front door to my childhood home, and my father has a slanted block of wood, the door stop, in his hand. Without his glasses, in the unlit hallway, he thinks I'm a burglar. He's going to stop me with a 3"-by-5" piece of wood. He squeezes the wood and gets a sliver in his palm, dropping the door stop on his shoes. (Dad as unlikely Cerberus.)

It's good to see you, Father, I say, although I've never in my life called him "Father."

There's no light on in the house. It's 4:00 in February and I want a lamp, a candle, or a fire to take the cold off the walls and out of the wooden floors. The windows are shut and the shades are drawn.

Don't track dirty snow into the house, he says. Go shake your shoes off outside. (Suddenly my dad is Martha Stewart? So, too, growing up in California, I didn't see snow until I went East to college.)

Random walls of snowdrifts rise out of the field, and in the dismal sun the trees reflect onto the snow like huge, broken umbrellas. The wind sweeps the snow off the ground, through the trees, and against the windows of the house.

In the living room, he rocks in his chair, with his feet on the stool. His hands are folded in his lap—a semi-feminine figure. He opens his mouth, but no words come out. Newspapers (containing articles he's written? I think so) are scattered across the floor. I sit away from him on the springs of a couch without cushions.

Under the glass tabletop next to him is a black-and-white picture of him hiking in the mountains with a walking stick in one hand, a pipe in the other. In the photograph, he is carrying a backpack and is half-turned toward the camera; in the photo, sunlight glamorizes his face. (The High Sierras: mountains of such magic importance to my childhood as to be commensurate with aboriginal promises of beauty and peace; jagged pinnacles far, far away, but so omnipresently in the mind.)

I open the window shade. Outside, to my surprise, it's twilight. The wind snaps twigs off the tree limbs. The snowdrifts are higher now.

Is the walkway clear? he asks.

The walkway from the porch to the driveway to the street is two feet deep in snow.

No, Father, I say. Why?

I'm expecting a letter, he says. (Implicitly, a letter from me.) Will you shovel the walkway?

I dig into the snowdrifts on either side of me. The weight of the shovel and a sudden gust of wind nearly make me fall. He stands behind the screen door, wearing a jacket so big he could use it as a sleeping bag. The pockets are at his knees and the hood is puffed out, framing his face—a skinny Jewish Eskimo.

I hit the blade against the ice, but it's frozen solid. He steps down off the porch, shuffling his feet until we get to the road, which is nearly a foot deep in snow. We trudge toward the post office at the end of the block. Frail as an old-age-home denizen, he holds on to my shoulder to prevent himself from falling.

The post office is an old brick building. Its cement steps are covered with snow, and its wooden door is halfway off its hinges. Inside are benches, a warped floor, and a couple hundred post office boxes: rose-colored glass rectangles with black numbers.

He takes off his coat and uses it as a pillow, kneeling on the floor and turning the dials of a box, rattling it until it opens. He beats his right hand against the sides.

The letter's been held up, he says, again. (I've failed, again.)

Outside, the sky is blankly black, the color of my gloves. Too cold to move, he clings to my arm. Ice gathers on his hood, forming a comical cap. He stops to cough, closing his eyes and breathing heavily. The return trip is always an exceedingly brief flash-forward. And there the dream ends.

Paradise, Soon Lost

Natalie celebrated her 10th birthday with 12 of her closest friends at Skate King, where the lights are low, the mirror ball glitters, the music crescendos every 30 seconds, and the bathrooms are labeled *Kings* and *Queens*. The girls, wearing rollerblades, seemed preternaturally tall, as if they were wearing high heels. My father had come up to Seattle from the Bay Area in honor of Natalie's big day, and at the party he mentioned to me that Natalie looked a little plump, her belly edging over her waistband; I asked him if he ever gave it a rest.

Several of Natalie's friends bought Best Friends split necklaces: one girl wears one half while her best friend wears the other. There was quite a competition for certain girls. Natalie's best friend, Amanda, asked the DJ to play a Michelle Branch song, and when it came on, Amanda beamed.

Seeing the lights go off, all of the younger girls rushed onto the rink. They liked the dark setting, which made them feel less noticeable, and yet Natalie and several of her friends were wearing orange glow sticks. So they didn't want their bodies to be noticed, but they did want their bodies to be noticed. This, I want to say, is the crux of the matter.

The girls skated backward. Then they skated in the regular

direction. After a while they did the limbo. The DJ played the standards: "I Will Survive," "Gloria," "YMCA," "Stayin' Alive," Madonna, the Black Eyed Peas, Avril Lavigne, Usher. Some of Natalie's friends bought plastic roses for themselves. Two teenaged kids were feverishly making out in a far corner. Duly noted by my father, who informed the management—quickly remedied. A quirky Puritanism: his abhorrence of any public display of affection. Whenever Laurie and I go to a movie with him, if I put my arm around her or hold her hand, he inevitably—and unconsciously, I think—erupts into a coughing fit until the PDA ceases.

As the father of a daughter who remains a Skate King devotee, I find the place utterly terrifying. It's all about amplifying kids' sense of themselves as magical creatures and converting this feeling into sexual yearning—a group march toward future prospects. For Natalie and her friends, still, just barely, the purpose of Skate King is to dream about the opposite sex without having to take these romantic feelings seriously, let alone act on them. In the dark, Natalie held Amanda's hand and lip-synched to Aaron Carter.

The last song of the afternoon was "The Hokey Pokey," which, the DJ explained to me, "adults don't care for." Of course adults (with the exception of my father, who wanted to join in until Natalie frantically waved him off) don't care for it; you wind up having to put your whole body in. What—Natalie and her friends were wondering—could that possibly consist of?

Girls develop breast buds between 8 and 10 years old, and full breasts between ages 12 and 18. Girls get their first pubic hair and armpit hair between ages 9 and 12, and they develop adult patterns of this hair between ages 13 and 14. I once heard statutory rape defended by the phrase "If there's grass on the field, play ball." In 1830, girls typically got their first period when they were 17. Thanks to improvements in nutrition, general health, and living conditions, the standard age in America is now 12 (12.75 in the 1960s, 12.5 in the early 1990s, and 12.3 early in this decade). Girls are getting fatter, which also helps trigger menstruation.

The average menstrual cycle is a little over 29 days. The moon's cycle of phases is 29.53 days. According to Darwin, menstruation is linked to the moon's influence on tidal rhythms, a legacy of our origin in the sea. For lemurs, estrus and sex tend to occur when there's a full moon.

At age 9 or 10, a boy's scrotum and testicles enlarge and his penis lengthens; at age 17, his penis has adult size and shape. Boys' pubic hair, armpit hair, leg hair, chest hair, and facial hair start at age 12, with adult patterns of the hair emerging at 15. First ejaculation usually occurs at age 12 or 13; at 14, most boys have a wet dream once every two weeks. I've forgotten the names of nearly everyone I went to junior high school with, but I'll never forget Pam Glinden or Joanne Liebes—best friends, bad girls, reputed "drug addicts"—to whose yearbook photos I masturbated throughout eighth grade. At the time, this activity seemed magical, private, perverse, unique, all-important. It wasn't. It was blood flowing through me which, at some point in the not entirely unforeseeable future (18,000 days, say, at the outside), will no longer flow. My dad will be dead soon; one day I'll be dead; despite—or perhaps because of—all the data gathered in this book, I still find those two facts overwhelming.

"The difference between sex and death," explains Woody Allen, "is that with death you can do it alone and no one's going to make fun of you."

Boys are heavier and taller than girls because they have a longer overall growth period. The growth spurt in boys occurs between 13 and 16; a gain of four inches can be expected in the peak year. For girls, the growth spurt begins at 11, may reach three inches in the peak year, and is almost completed by 14. At 18, three-quarters of an inch of growth remains for boys and slightly less for girls, for whom growth is 99 percent complete. Between ages 15 and 18, I grew from 5'4" to 6'1"; I still visualize myself being small. Natalie, shorter than most of her classmates, is mad at me for not having my growth spurt until the end of high school. She can't wait to "stretch out."

When Natalie was 2, Laurie and I were putting on Natalie's clothes to take her to day care. My father was visiting for the week. Natalie cried frantically, complaining that the clothes were the wrong clothes—this was the wrong color, that was too tight. She kept saying, "Mine, mine, mine." Afterward, I asked my dad what he thought Natalie was trying to tell us, and he said, "She meant, 'These limbs, these legs, these arms: they're mine. Don't do this to my body. It's my body.'" I asked him if I ever did stuff like that as a kid, and he said, "Are you kidding? You drove me and your mother up a wall, especially that first year. What a crybaby!"

News Flash: We Are Animals

My friend Suzanne e-mailed me about her daughter: "Naomi is nine now, edging up to those perilous years, and while I realize that some awkwardness is inevitable for teenagers, I sense that for girls the body-confidence that is lost is often lost for good. I keep this image of Naomi in my mind: when she comes home from school, she likes to grab a yogurt from the fridge and eat it out on the deck while she hula hoops. She uses two hula hoops at once and she'll stand practically still, barely twitching her nonexistent hips, spooning yogurt into her mouth and telling me about her day. The hula hoops spin around her as smoothly as satellites, as if there is some intense gravitational pull coming from inside of her. This ritual never ceases to leave me gaping in astonishment and gratitude. Where does this grace come from? My hunch is that her utter lack of self-consciousness about the pleasure it gives her to move her body renders her incredibly graceful. She has an anthem that I love. She'll approach me very seriously and say, 'Mom. *Mom.* I have to tell you something.' She locks me into a deep stare and then suddenly she's bouncing up and down in a dance that's all knees and elbows, singing, 'There's a little bit of frog in all of us, no matter who you be!'"

. . .

When Natalie was 11, panda bears (sad-eyed, sedentary, round: cute) were her favorite things in existence. She made a board game entitled I'm Outta the Pound!: pets escape the pound and try to find a home. "Sex must be an okay thing," she told me, "because people have sex to produce more life." She still does stunningly accurate imitations of animals.

My favorite moment of Natalie's weekly soccer game occurs when the game is over, the parents are handing out snacks, and all the girls are sitting in a circle, not really talking much but drinking their juices and eating their cookies, enjoying their bodies' exhaustion, utterly in tune with themselves and one another. Sometimes my dad will be there and he'll stop taking pictures for a minute and, his eyes misting, he'll just revel and kvell in the moment, the fact and glory of physical existence.

Hoop dream (i):

There has always been some strange connection for me between basketball and the dark. I started shooting baskets after school in third grade, and I remember dusk and macadam combining into the sensation that the world was dying but I was indestructible. One afternoon I played H-O-R-S-E with a classmate, Renée Hahn, who threw the ball over the fence and said, "I don't want to play with you anymore. You're too good. I'll bet one day you're going to be a San Francisco Warrior."

Renée had a way of moving her body like a boy but still like a girl, too, and that game of H-O-R-S-E is one of the happiest memories of my childhood: dribbling around in the dark but knowing by instinct where the basket was; not being able to see Renée but smelling her sweat and keeping close to her voice, in which I could hear her love for me and my life as a Warrior opening up into the night. I remember the sloped half-court at the far end of the playground, its orange pole, orange rim, and wooden green backboard, the chain net clanging in the wind, the sand on the court, the overhanging eucalyptus trees, the fence the ball bounced over into the street, and the bench the girls sat on, watching, trying to look bored.

The first two weeks of summer, Renée and I went steady, but we broke up when I didn't risk rescuing her in a game of Capture the Flag, so she wasn't around for my 10th birthday. I begged my parents to let Ethan Saunders, Jim Morrow, Bradley Gamble, and me shoot baskets by ourselves all night at the court across the street. My mother and father reluctantly agreed, and my father swung by every few hours to make sure we were safe and bring more Coke, more birthday cake, more candy.

Near midnight, Bradley and I were playing two-on-two against Jim and Ethan. The moon was falling. We had a lot of sugar in our blood, and all of us were totally zonked and totally wired. With the score tied at 18 in a game to 20, I took a very long shot from the deepest corner. Before the ball had even left my hand, Bradley said, "Way to hit."

I was a good shooter because it was the only thing I ever did, and I did it all the time, but even for me such a shot was doubtful. Still, Bradley knew and I knew and Jim and Ethan knew, too, and we knew the way we knew our own names or the batting averages of the Giants' starting lineup or the life-lines in our palms. I felt it in my legs and up my spine, which arched as I fell back. My fingers tingled and my hand squeezed the night in joyful follow-through. We knew the shot was per-

fect: when we heard the ball (a birthday present from my
father) whip through the net, we heard it as something we had
already known for at least a second. What happened in that
second during which we knew? Did the world stop? Did my
soul ascend a couple of notches? What happens to ESP, to such
keen eyesight? What did we have then, anyway, radar? When
did we have to start working so hard to hear our own hearts?

At the end of J. M. Coetzee's novel *Elizabeth Costello*, the only
thing the eponymous elderly protagonist can affirm is not love
or art or religion but the sound of frogs, trapped in mud,
belling with the cessation of torrential rain. Nietzsche: "There
is more wisdom in your body than in your deepest philoso-
phy." Wittgenstein said, "Our only certainty is to act with the
body." Martha Graham: "The body never lies." We are all
thrillingly different animals, and we are all, in a sense, the same
animal. The body—in its movement from swaddling to casket—can tell us everything we can possibly know about everything.

Motherhood

At the Alaska SeaLife Center, Aurora, a Giant Pacific female octopus, was introduced to J-1, a male octopus. They flashed colors and retreated to a dark corner of the center's "Denizens of the Deep" display. A month later, Aurora laid thousands of eggs. Despite the fact that her eggs didn't appear to develop and aquarists—the animals' caretakers—believed the eggs were sterile, Aurora daily sucked in water through her mantle and sent cleansing waves over the eggs, defending them against hungry sea cucumbers and starfish. Even when aquarists, certain the eggs weren't fertile, began draining her 3,600-gallon tank, Aurora sprayed her eggs, exposed and drying on rocks. Several eggs from Aurora hatched exactly 10 months after her encounter with J-1 (long since deceased); nine baby octopi received food through an electronic, automatic feeder in a rearing tank. Although Giant Pacific females usually die about the same time as their eggs hatch, mostly because they stop eating for months and spend their energy defending their eggs, aquarist Ed DeCastro said Aurora appeared invigorated and that "she was still tending the eggs."

. . .

In seventh grade, Natalie suddenly loved to criticize Laurie for getting a point of information wrong or having pieces of food caught between her teeth or chewing too loudly or, especially, talking while eating. These were, I now know, the opening fisticuffs of the apparently inexorable mother-daughter donnybrook that will dominate our house for the next several years.

My father takes a variety of medications to combat anxiety, depression, and sleeplessness. Earlier this year, he and I visited his psychiatrist to make sure that he was taking them in the right combination. We had a few extra minutes at the end of the session, so I asked my father's very Freudian psychiatrist why teenage daughters are so critical of their mothers. He said, "All that hormonal energy is coursing madly through a daughter's body, and it becomes, for various reasons, anger at the mother. I think the daughter unconsciously senses the tremendous leverage the onset of her fertility gives her, which causes the family to start treating her with more deference. She's the chance for the family to perpetuate itself. Her mother's leaving this arena just as the daughter's entering it. When they study this issue, disputes between mothers and daughters, not only does the father invariably side with the daughter"—I can't remember my father ever doing this with my sister; my mother ruled the roost, regardless—"but so does everybody else. The genes are driving the family to protect the most fertile female. So a good deal of a girl's anger at her mother has to do with the mixture of power she feels with the onset of fertility and the burden she feels at being the designated bearer of children." My dad sat next to me, listening to this, nodding and mmm-huhing, elbowing me in the ribs at appropriate moments, proud of his shrink's Olympian overview.

The Actuarial Prime of Life, or Why Children Don't Like Spicy Food

Tolstoy, in his late 70s, said, "As I was at five, so I am now." St. Ignatius Loyola said, "Give me the child until he is seven, and I will show you the man." Wordsworth wrote, "The Child is father of the Man." Is the father the father of the man as well? I suppose he must be.

Aging begins immediately after the actuarial prime of life. In the United States and in most other developed countries, the actuarial prime of life is age 7. After you turn 7, your risk of dying doubles every eight years.

By the time you're 5, your head has attained 90 percent of its mature size. By age 7, your brain reaches 90 percent of its maximum weight; by 9, 95 percent; during adolescence, 100 percent. Two percent of total body weight and 60 percent fat, the brain receives 20 percent of the blood coming from the heart and consumes 20 percent of all the oxygen in the body.

Between ages 5 and 10, your kidneys double in size to keep up with the increased metabolic wastes of the body. At ages 6 and 7, lymphoid tissues, which produce antibodies, reach their peak size.

A toddler's stomach is the shape of a cow's horn; at 9, it's the shape of a fish hook; at 12, it's the shape of a bagpipe and has achieved functional maturity.

The average duration of a 6- to 10-year-old's activity is six seconds for low-intensity activities and three seconds for high-intensity activities. "At ten," Schopenhauer said, "Mercury is in the ascendant; at that age, a youth, like this planet, is characterized by extreme mobility within a narrow sphere, where trifles have a great effect upon him." This is a perfect description of my father as he is and as he always has been: a perpetual 10-year-old.

Growth from birth to adolescence occurs in two distinct patterns: the first, from birth to 2 years, is one of rapid but decelerating growth; the second, from 2 years to the onset of puberty, is one of more consistent annual increments. An average 1-year-old is 30 inches tall, a 2-year-old is 35 inches, a 4-year-old is 40 inches, and an 8-year-old is 50 inches. During the elementary school years, children's growth slows to about two inches a year. Your height relative to your peers usually doesn't change much after age 6, and the proportions of your weight tend to remain the same as well.

Weight increase follows a similar curve. An infant doubles his or her birth weight by 5 months, triples it by 1 year, and quadruples it by 2 years. Between ages 2 and 5, you gain about the same amount of weight each year: four to five pounds. Between ages 6 and 10, your growth levels off—a lull between the rapid growth of early childhood and prepubescence. During these years, you gain about five to seven pounds per year.

Between ages 6 and 11 your head appears to enlarge, and your facial features exhibit significant changes, because of the growth of your facial bones. Your face literally grows away or out from its skull.

By age 5, the heart has quadrupled its birth size. At age 9, it's six times its birth weight, and by puberty it's almost ten times its birth weight. As the heart grows, it assumes a more vertical position within the thoracic cavity. The diaphragm descends, allowing more room for both cardiac action and respiratory expansion.

When you're born, taste buds cover your mouth, with flavor sensors on the roof of your mouth, your throat, and the lateral surface of your tongue—which is why most very young children don't like spicy food. The entire top of their oval cavity is covered with taste buds; for young children, tasting Tabasco sauce is an entirely different experience than it is for an adult. By the time you're 10, most of these extra taste buds are gone.

The ability to exactly duplicate foreign sounds disappears after age 12.

Two to four years before puberty, most children have already attained 75 to 80 percent of their adult height and 50 percent of their adult weight. Just before the onset of puberty, the shaft and ends of your "long bones" (femur, tibia, fibula) fuse: the maturation of the skeletal system and that of the reproductive system are perfectly synchronized. What fearful symmetry to our mortal frame.

Nobody knows what causes puberty to begin.

Sex and Death (i)

Every once in a while, an egg cell becomes activated while it's still in the ovary and starts to develop all on its own. The result, in mammals, is a teratoma. (The sperm-forming cells of the testis also produce teratomas on occasion.) The egg divides and begins the early stages of embryogenesis seemingly normally, but it fails to complete the proper developmental sequence. The embryo forms a shapeless mass of cells containing a variety of different cell types and partly formed organs: bones, skin, bits of glands, and even hair.

A teratoma can develop into a teratocarcinoma, a life-threatening cancer that will, when transplanted—in a lab experiment—from animal to animal of the same genetic strain, grow without limit until it kills its host. However, if some cells are taken from the teratocarcinoma of, for example, a mouse, and if these cancerous cells are then injected into an early-stage mouse embryo, the resulting animal will be entirely normal: the teratocarcinoma cells will be tamed by the developmental signals being produced in the early-stage embryo.

In other words, cancer cells can behave very much like the cells of an early embryo. Many of the genes responsible for cancer late in life are intimately involved in the regulation of cell growth and differentiation early in life. The genes that have such devastating effects late in life when expressed in diseases such as Alzheimer's seem to be identical to their early life form, when they serve a useful function. In a teratocarcinoma, the germ cells become a voracious parasite of the body. The balance is lost between the goals of the body (preserving health and life) and the goals of the germ cells (reproduction).

For every cell, there's a time to live and a time to die. Cells can die by injury or by suicide. The pattern of events in death by suicide is so orderly that the process is often called "programmed cell death," which destroys cells that represent a threat to the integrity of the organism—for instance, cells infected with viruses, cells with DNA damage, or cancer cells. Dylan Thomas wrote (I love this line and my father abhors it),

> *The force that through the green fuse drives the flower*
> *Drives my green age; that blasts the roots of trees*
> *Is my destroyer.*

Hoop Dream (ii)

As members of the Borel Middle School Bobcats, we worked out in a tiny gym with loose buckets and slippery linoleum and butcher-paper posters exhorting us toward conquest. I remember late practices full of wind sprints and tipping drills. One day the coach said, "Okay, gang, let me show you how we're gonna run picks for Dave." My friends ran around the court, passing, cutting, and screening for me. All for me. Set-plays for me to shoot from the top of the circle or the left corner—my favorite spots. It felt like the whole world was weaving to protect me, then release me.

That summer, my father had been fired from his job as publicity director for the Jewish Welfare Federation and accepted a much lower-paying job as director of the poverty program of San Mateo County. He sat in a one-room office without air-conditioning and called grocery stores, wanting to know why they didn't honor food stamps; called restaurants, asking if, as the signs in the windows proclaimed, they were indeed equal opportunity employers. Sometimes, on weekends, he flew to Sacramento or Washington to request more money for his program. Watts rioted; Detroit burned. His constituents worshipped him. He said, "Please. I'm just doing my job." They called him the Great White Hope and invited him to barbecues, weddings, softball games. At the softball games he outplayed everybody. The salary was $7,500 a year, but he was happy. The ghetto was his.

After school I'd walk across town, leave my books in my father's office, then go around the block to play basketball with black kids. I developed a double-pump jump shot, which among the eighth graders I went to school with was unheard of. Rather than shooting on the way up, I tucked my knees, hung in the air a second, pinwheeled the ball, then shot on the way down. My white friends hated my new move. It seemed tough, mannered, teenaged, vaguely Negro. The more I shot like this, the more my white friends disliked me, and the more they disliked me, the more I shot like this. At the year-end assembly, I was named "best athlete," and my father said that when I went up to accept the trophy, I even walked like a jock. At the time, I took this as gentle mockery, although I realize now he meant it as the ultimate accolade.

From kindergarten through eighth grade all I really did was play sports, think about sports, dream about sports. I learned to read by devouring mini-bios of jock stars. I learned math by computing players' averages (and my own). At 12 I ran the 50-yard dash in six seconds, which caused kids from all over the city to come to my school and race me. During a five-on-five weave drill at a summer basketball camp, the director of the camp, a recently retired professional basketball player, got called over to watch how accurately I could throw passes behind my back; he said he could have used a point guard like me when he was playing, and he bumped me up out of my grade level. I remember once hitting a home run in the bottom of the 12th inning to win a Little League All-Star game, then coming home to lie down in my uniform in the hammock in our backyard, drink lemonade, eat sugar cookies, and measure my accomplishments against the fellows featured in the just-arrived issue of *Sports Illustrated*. Christ, I remember thinking, how could life possibly get any better than this?

A little too often my father likes to quote the line "Backward, turn backward, O Time, in your flight, / Make me a child again just for to-night!" Here he is, turning backward: "School always excited me. Easy to understand why: I was a pretty good mixer, had few 'bad' days. I knew how to read when I entered first grade; my three older brothers, especially Phil, a columnist for the *New York Sun*, had seen to that. Learning how to spell was a never-ending source of delight and wonderment; it still is. And I did well after school on the running track and the softball diamond. I got a big charge out of competing against—and usually beating—my fellow students. Soon, I had friends who wanted to bask in my reflected glory."

When he was in his mid-20s, he attended an open tryout with the Brooklyn Dodgers and lasted all the way to the final round, when someone named Van Lingle Mungo hit every pitch my father threw—onto Bedford Avenue. Undeniably, I inherited my athletic genes from him. When Natalie assisted on the goal that won her soccer team the city championship, he crowed, "The Shields bloodline!"

Bloodline to Star Power (i)

My father's birth certificate reads "Milton Shildcrout." His military record says "Milton P. Schildcrout" (he had no middle name; he made it up). When he changed his name in 1946 to "Shields," the petition listed both "Shildkrout" and "Shildkraut." His brother Abe used "Shildkrout"; his sister Fay's maiden name was "Schildkraut." Who cares? I do. I want to know whether I'm related to Joseph Schildkraut, who played Otto Frank in *The Diary of Anne Frank* and won an Academy Award in 1938 for his portrayal of Alfred Dreyfus in *The Life of Emile Zola*.

I grew up under the distinct impression that it was simply true—the actor was my father's cousin—but now my father is considerably more equivocal: "There is the possibility that we're related," he'll say, "but I wouldn't know how to establish it." Or: "Do I have definite proof that he was a cousin of ours? No." Or: "My brother Jack bore a strong resemblance to him; he really did." From a letter: "Are we really related, the two families? Can't say for certain. What's the legend I've fashioned over the years and what's solid, indisputable fact? I don't know." "We could be related to the Rudolph/Joseph Schildkraut family—I honestly believe that."

37

In 1923, when my father was 13, his father, Samuel, took him to a Yiddish theater on the Lower East Side to see Rudolph Schildkraut substitute for the legendary Jacob Adler in the lead role of a play called *Der Vilder Mensch* (*The Wild Man*). Rudolph was such a wild man: he hurtled himself, gripping a rope, from one side of the stage to the other. After the play, which was a benefit performance for my grandfather's union—the International Ladies Garment Workers—my grandfather convinced the guard that he was related to Rudolph Schildkraut, and he and my father went backstage.

In a tiny dressing room, Rudolph removed his makeup and stage costume, and he and Samuel talked. According to my father, Rudolph said he was born in Romania, and later in his acting career he went to Vienna and Berlin. ("Schildkraut" is of German-Russian derivation. "Schild" means "shield"; "kraut" means "cabbage." We're protectors and defenders of cabbage.) He and his wife and son, Joseph, came to New York around 1910, went back to Berlin a few years later, and then returned to the United States permanently in 1920. (Joseph Schildkraut's 1959 memoir, *My Father and I*, confirms that these dates are correct, which only proves that my father probably consulted the book before telling me the story.) Samuel asked Rudolph whether he knew anything about his family's antecedents—how and when they came to Austria. Rudolph said he knew little or nothing. His life as an actor took him to many places, and his life and interest were the theater and its people. The two men spoke in Yiddish for about 10 minutes; my father and grandfather left. What little my father couldn't understand, my grandfather explained to him later.

"For weeks," my father told me, "I regaled my friends and anybody who would listen that my father and I had visited the great star of the Austrian, German, and Yiddish theater in

America—Rudolph Schildkraut. What's more, I said, he was probably our cousin. Nothing in the conversation between my father and Rudolph Schildkraut would lead me or anybody else to come to that conclusion for a certainty, but I wanted to impress friends and neighbors and quickly added Rudolph and Joseph Schildkraut to our family. I said, 'They're probably second cousins.' Some days I made them 'first cousins.' Rudolph Schildkraut—as you know, Dave—went on to Hollywood and had a brief but successful motion picture career. I told everybody he was a much better actor than his countryman Emil Jannings."

Adolescence

Rattlesnake Lake

Testosterone initiates the growth spurt; increases larynx size, deepening the voice; increases red blood cell mass, muscle mass, libido; stimulates development of the penis, scrotum, and prostate; stimulates growth of pubic, facial, leg, and armpit hair; stimulates sebaceous gland secretions of oil. Throughout high school, my acne was so severe as to constitute a second skin. Oil leaked from my pores. I kissed no one until I was 17.

Acne flourished on my chin, forehead, cheeks, temples, and scalp, and behind my ears. It burned my neck, appeared sporadically on my penis, visited my stomach, and wrapped around my back and buttocks. It was like an unwilling, monotonous tattoo. There were whiteheads on the nose, blackheads on toes, dense purple collections that finally burst with blood, white circles that vanished in a squeeze, dilating welts that never went away, infected wounds that cut to the bone, surface scars that looked hideous, wart-like protuberances at the side of the head. I endured collagen injections, punch grafts, and chemical peels.

I washed with oval brown bars and transparent green squares, soft baby soaps that sudsed, and rough soaps that burned. I applied special gels, clear white liquids, mud creams.

I took tablets once, twice, thrice a day; before, after, and during meals. I went on milk diets and no-milk diets, absorbed no sun and too much sun. I took erythromycin, tretinoin, Cleocin, PanOxyl, Benoxyl, isopropyl myristate, polyoxyl 40 stearate, butylated hydroxytoluene, hydroxypropyl methylcellulose. I saw doctors and doctors and doctors.

My father would ask me, please, to stop picking at myself. Sometimes he'd get impatient and slap my face (as if he were both reprimanding me for squeezing scabs at the dinner table and expressing compassion by striking the source of all the distress), but he was certainly justified in whatever frustration he felt. My hands were incessantly crawling across my skin, always probing and plucking, then flicking away the root canker. The inflammatory disease bred a weird narcissism in which I craved the mirror but averted any accurate reflection. I became expert at predicting which kinds of mirrors would soften the effect, and which—it hardly seemed possible—would make things worse.

My mother still had pockmarks on her cheeks as evidence of a diseased childhood, with patches of pink skin on her nose acquired in more than one surgery to remove the skin cancer that was her reward for believing, as a teenager, too many doctors' X-ray radiation cures. (The enormous amount of radiation she received was thought to be the likely cause of her breast cancer and death at 51.) In a faded photograph of her brother wearing khaki in Okinawa, his face appeared to be on fire. A doctor at Stanford Hospital told my sister that he was the most decorated dermatologist in the Bay Area and there wasn't a thing he could do to improve the quality of her skin until she was at least 21. Only my father's face was impressively blemish-free, although whenever he cut himself shaving or the impress of his glasses left a red mark at the eyebrows, my mother would claim that he, too, had had problems. They used to have perfectly absurd arguments over who was responsible for the cluster forming on my chin.

My sophomore year of high school my zit trouble reached such catastrophic proportions that twice a month I drove an hour each way to receive liquid nitrogen treatments from a dermatologist in South San Francisco. His office was catty-corner to a shopping center that housed a Longs drugstore, where I would always first give my prescription for that month's miracle drug to the pharmacist. Then, while I was waiting for the prescription to be filled, I'd go buy a giant bag of Switzer's red licorice. I'd tear open the bag, and even if (especially if) my face was still bleeding slightly from all the violence that had just been done to it, I'd start gobbling the licorice while standing in line for the cashier. I'm hard-pressed now to see the licorice as anything other than some sort of Communion wafer, as if by swallowing the licorice, my juicy red pimples might become sweet and tasty. I'd absorb them; I'd be absolved. The purity of the contradiction I remember as a kind of ecstasy. My senior yearbook photo was so airbrushed that people asked me, literally, who it was.

In "Is Acne Really a Disease?" Dale F. Bloom argues that, "far from being a disease, adolescent acne is a normal physiological process that functions to ward off potential mates until the afflicted individual is some years past the age of reproductive maturity, and thus emotionally, intellectually, and physically fit to be a parent." Dale F. Bloom's thesis seems to me unassailable.

In one study, of teenage boys with the highest testosterone levels, 69 percent said they'd had intercourse; of boys with the lowest levels, 16 percent said they'd had intercourse. The testosterone level in boys is eight times that of girls. Testosterone is responsible for increasing boys' muscle mass and initiating the growth spurt, which peaks at age 14. From ages 11 to 16, boys' testosterone levels increase 20-fold. By age 16, the cardiovascular system has established its adult size and rhythm.

Hair grows about half an inch a month; it grows fastest in young adults, and fastest of all in girls between ages 16 and 24. Brain scans of people processing a romantic gaze, new mothers listening to infant cries, and subjects under the influence of cocaine bear a striking resemblance to one another. According to Daniel McNeill, "Our pupils reach peak size in adolescence, almost certainly as a lure in love, then slowly contract till age sixty." As Natalie would say—as she actually did say—"That's awesome."

When she asked me why people write graffiti, I tried to explain how teenage boys need to ruin what's there in order to become who they are. I talked about boys at the swimming pool who simply wouldn't obey the pleasant female lifeguard asking them to leave the pool at closing time; they left only when asked gruffly by the male African-American lifeguard, and then they left immediately.

"One Sunday morning," my father reminisced to me over the phone, "my father announced that he was going out to watch me play punchball. That was the first time in all the years I'd been playing that he expressed a desire to see me play. We played in the street in front of my house. The only interruptions came when a horse and buggy came through. My father found a place to watch at the left-field foul line. I saw him standing there and waved as I took my turn to hit. This time, I hit the 'Spaldeen'—that's what we called the Spalding high bouncer—with all my might and it shot like an arrow for the very spot where my father was standing, going probably sixty miles an hour. My father stood there, waving at the ball futilely. It struck him on his left cheek, missed his eye by inches."

According to Boyd McCandless, "A youngster *is* his body and his body is *he*."

Tolstoy said, "I have read somewhere that children from twelve to fourteen years of age—that is, in the transition stage from childhood to adolescence—are singularly inclined to arson and even murder. As I look back upon my boyhood, I can quite appreciate the possibility of the most frightful crime being committed without object or intent to injure but *just because*—out of curiosity, or to satisfy an unconscious craving for action."

A dozen or so teenage boys stood atop a jagged rock in the middle of Rattlesnake Lake, four miles southeast of North Bend, an hour out of Seattle. Several teenage girls did the same. I lazed about on a raft, watching from afar. The boys wore cutoffs and, nearly without exception, boasted chiseled chests. The girls, wearing cutoffs and bikini tops, seemed considerably less toned. (During the pubescent growth spurt, girls' hips widen in relation to shoulder girth. Boys' shoulders widen in relation to hip width. Eighteen-year-old girls have 20 percent less bone mass in relation to body weight than boys of the same age.)

The rock was perhaps one story high. The boys chose to dive from the higher parts of the rock into the lake; most of the girls dove, too, but less spectacularly, less dangerously. One girl who didn't dive kept being pestered by her friend: "I can't believe you're seventeen and you won't dive. If you don't, I'm never going to speak to you again."

The boys at Rattlesnake Lake kept asking one another about their own dives, "How was that one? How did that look?"

It looks like this: the average penis of a man is 3″ to 4″ when flaccid and 5″ to 7″ when erect. The recorded range for an erect penis is 3.75″ to 9.6″. In the 1930s, mannequins imported from Europe came in three sizes according to the size of the genitalia: small, medium, and American (compared to other cultures, Americans are obsessed with the size of sexual organs: penises, breasts). Lyndon Johnson frequently urinated in front of his secretary, routinely forced staff members to meet with him in the bathroom while he defecated, and liked to show off his penis, which he nicknamed "Jumbo"; in a private conversation, pressed by a couple of reporters to explain why we were in Vietnam, LBJ unzipped his fly, displayed Jumbo, and said, "This is why." Phallocrypts, sheaths that cover a New Guinean man's penis, run to two feet in length. The length of my penis when erect is 6″ (boringly, frustratingly average); I've measured it several times. My father, though much smaller overall than I am, is, I'm pretty sure (glimpsed discreetly), markedly more well-endowed. No wonder he used to be such a sex fiend.

Boys vs. Girls (ii)

At birth, body fat is 12 percent of body weight, increases to 25 percent at 6 months, and 30 percent at 1 year. At age 6, it's back down to 12 percent again, then it rises until the onset of puberty. Postpuberty, the rise continues in girls, while in boys there's a slight decline.

During high school, girls' bone development is 2 years ahead of boys. Young girls surpass boys in height and weight, and they frequently remain taller until boys enter the adolescent growth spurt that accompanies pubescence. Maximum skeletal development occurs at 16 for most girls and 19 for boys; dating between classmates in high school is by definition a hormonal mismatch and a farce.

"At seventeen, you tend to go in for unhappy love affairs," said Françoise Sagan, who should know.

In males, the sexual urge peaks during their late teens or early twenties, but not until a decade later does it peak in females.

"I would there were no age between sixteen and three-and-twenty, / or that youth would sleep out the rest; / for there is nothing in the between / but getting wenches / with child, wronging the ancientry, stealing, fighting"—so saith the Shepherd in *The Winter's Tale*.

Between ages 15 and 24, men are three times more likely to die than women, mostly by reckless behavior or violence—e.g., murder, suicide, car accidents, war.

F. Scott Fitzgerald wrote to his daughter, Scottie, "For premature adventure one pays an atrocious price. As I told you once, every boy who drank at eighteen or nineteen is now safe in his grave."

Hoop dream (iii):

My father was the manager of a semi-pro basketball team called the Brooklyn Eagles, which consisted of Harry Glatzer; his brother, Nat, who played for Thomas Jefferson—where they both went to high school—"but," according to my father, "went nowhere following graduation"; Max "Puzzy" Posnack, at the time the captain of St. John's; Allie Schuckman, also a star at St. John's; Max "Kappy" Kaplan, from St. John's as well; Artie Jackson, a black player who displayed "dazzling accuracy from all over the floor"; and Isador "Midge" Serota, who "filled his days playing pickup basketball." The Eagles were to be paid $100 under the table (since many of the players were college athletes) to provide the opposition for a Christmas Day game at Yale.

There is, I'm sure, much mythmaking in my father's version of the story (and all his stories); the last time he told me this story, he told it with the same, implausibly perfect details he always does: as he and the seven players drove from Brooklyn to New Haven, "a slight snowfall came down at about four or five o'clock P.M., making driving a little tricky, but Kappy was a good driver. Somewhere, about twenty-five or thirty miles from New Haven, the light snowfall turned heavier, making driving a little dangerous. We were making slow but steady progress toward our goal, the Yale basketball court.

"All of a sudden, we felt a bump against the front fender. A body rolled up over the fender and off the car onto the roadway. We'd hit a man. We stopped the car, raced to a nearby farmhouse, and called the local sheriff, who showed up in about fifteen minutes and started asking Kappy if he'd been drinking or driving too fast, especially under these hazardous conditions. One look at the body by the sheriff and he said, 'It's that old Polack, the town drunk. He probably never saw you.'

"We were watching the time. We had to be in New Haven by six-thirty. The sheriff told us about a farmer who lived nearby and did commercial driving. By this time—five-thirty or so—we had to skip dinner, hire the farmer-driver for twenty dollars, and get to the game. Kappy's car was impounded as evidence and would have to be kept in the town of Wilton, where we hit the man. We piled into the big limousine and got to the gym about seven, cold and hungry. The Yale people, who thought they'd been stood up, were furious with us.

"We changed into our uniforms, had a brief warm-up, and the first quarter ended with the Yalies leading by twenty points; the half ended with Yale up about thirty. At halftime, Allie and the team gulped down sandwiches and sodas. Hardly the recommended diet for players engaged in a clash with finely trained athletes—rested and ready for the game against those 'tough guys' from Brooklyn. Puzzy gave the team a pep talk at halftime and the second half was a different story.

"Puzzy, Allie, and Artie began hitting their shots. The game ended in a tie. We played two overtimes and lost by a basket. The Yale captain thanked us and paid me the hundred dollars, twenty of which immediately went to the farmer-driver to drive us back to the bus station in Wilton. We got on board the bus around midnight and arrived back in New York at about six A.M. The players made a dash for the Automat (now defunct; you placed nickels in food slots, and out came the food, from main dishes to dessert). I distributed what was left: each player got a few bucks. I took nothing. We had enough for subway fare—five cents back to Brooklyn—and the game was history. It soon became a neighborhood legend.

"A month later, Kappy went back to Wilton for the inquest. He was declared innocent. We never played another game."

Why Lionesses Prefer Dark Brunettes, or Why Both Men and Women Are Attracted to Deep Voices

The olfactory system—the sense of smell—bypasses all the brain's thinking processes and directs its information exclusively toward the regions that control sex and aggression. In order to mate with a female hamster, male hamsters must have this system functioning. Male mice need it in order to respond to female fertility signals, and female pigs need it to be aroused by boars. In humans, scent no longer dominates sexual response; scent is nowhere near as significant for us as it is for the rest of the animal kingdom.

Sight is much the most important human sense; appearance is what attracts us. "Gentlemen prefer blondes," but lionesses prefer dark brunettes, which are believed to have higher testosterone levels and potentially better genes.

Humans and many other species find voices attractive. In humans, deep, husky voices—considered sexually attractive by both sexes—are also correlated with high testosterone levels and therefore potentially high sex drive and good genes.

Fear and terror, not shared pleasant experiences, are more likely to result in mutual attraction. The release of stress hormones activates the brain's neurochemical systems that promote attachment bonds. In a famous experiment, an attractive woman interviewed young men on a swaying rope bridge 200 feet above a river, and also on the ground. Midway through the interview, she gave them her phone number. Over 60 percent of the men she interviewed on the rope bridge called her back; only 30 percent of the men on the ground did so.

I was 17, as was my girlfriend, Carla, and neither of us was sexually experienced. Rain fell like needles, but Carla's parents' cabin's back porch, sheltered by a lean-to roof and enclosed by a tight green net, kept us dry. I wanted to sleep outside, catch cold. I wanted to share disease and shudder. Carla wanted to brush her teeth. She liked the smell of bathrooms, mirrors, warm toilet seats. Toothbrush and towel in hand, she pushed open the screen door and sought linoleum.

I unfolded the sleeping bags and unrolled them on the wooden floor, fluffing up our backpacks, tucking them into the mouths of the sleeping bags. I pushed the bench out of the way into the corner of the porch. I rearranged things and waited.

"Everything's wet out here," Carla said when she emerged. "Let's sleep inside."

"No," I said. "The rain'll stop soon."

I shut the door to the house, jiggled the doorknob, and pronounced the door locked. The only way to get in was to find the key somewhere on the porch come morning.

Carla got under the covers and lay down next to me in her sleeping bag.

"How do I look?" she asked.

I searched my mind for adjectives. I wanted to please her, choose the right ones by being descriptive. "Kissable. Dreamy. Exquisite."

"H-H-How do I look?" I asked. I stuttered less when I was alone with Carla than I did with anyone else, but it still cropped up occasionally.

Carla laughed and avoided the question. Whenever she asked me how she looked, she knew that whatever I answered, she was irresistible. She wanted me to be handsome, but I wasn't. My pimples wouldn't go away; I wouldn't go away. I was who I was. I wasn't handsome. Carla knew that. She could see. She wasn't blind. She loved me, nevertheless. She loved me for the complexity of my soul—something like that. Anyone can have clear skin (as my father does), blue eyes (ditto), wavy hair (till middle age), a mellifluous voice (still).

We touched fingertips, interlocked fingers, pressed palms together like flat stomachs, squeezed tight. I spread her middle fingers, moved my index finger up and back between her fingers. I held the back of her neck, closed my eyes, kissed her. Surprisingly, she sat up, kissed me, and then we bumped foreheads while I was undoing the zipper of my sleeping bag and sliding closer to her. She laughed at what she took to be my clumsiness. I kissed her pug nose. We joined lips and twisted our heads until I said, "We're destined to make love tonight."

"I don't know," she said. "I'm not sure I'm ready. It's cold. I really need to use the bathroom first."

She got out of her sleeping bag, gathered up a few things from her backpack, tried the door.

"It's locked," I said.

She turned the doorknob, pushed the door open.

"Liar," she said.

"I honestly thought I'd locked the door," I said.

She closed the door softly behind her while I lay down on the sleeping bag. Outside, tree limbs swayed like broken arms and thick sheets of cutting rain erased the sky. I waited for

Carla, who could easily be another few hours. She got lost in bathrooms. She felt safe in them, at home, locked in. She had a toilet kit like a suitcase. She liked to be clean. She talked about towels and soaps and different kinds of tissues—their warmth, their softness. She liked to play with faucets. Trans-fixed on beauty, she stared into mirrors for hours, scared away blemishes.

I was, in a sense and for the moment, one of those blem-ishes: I wasn't Carla's dream boy. I didn't have a deep, husky voice. I wasn't the lioness's dark brunette.

My father, reminiscing to me recently about his first girlfriend, said, "For about five years, from the time I was twenty-three until twenty-eight, I dated one of your Aunt Fay's friends, Pearl Feinberg, a tall and very attractive young woman whose stat-uesque figure evoked appreciative whistles and oohs and aahs from onlookers. (Don't think we called it 'dating' back then, but you know what I mean.) Pearl was employed as a secretary and part-time model for one of New York's big apparel firms. I had a good job (working for the *Journal-American*), a lovely girlfriend, a knock-your-eyes-out tan Ford convertible (which looked like today's VW Cabriolet), some money. I felt like I had the whole world in my twenty-five-year-old hands.

"Pearl and I were always busy when we saw each other on the weekends: the movies, the theater, picnics, parties, lectures, and tennis in nearby Highland Park. Although we dated steadily for five years—all our friends expected us to be together forever—we never talked marriage. The fault was mostly mine. We were both well past the age of consent, but I was too immature, afraid to the point of being phobic about taking on responsibility. I was the least sophisticated twenty-eight-year-old in the Western Hemisphere.

"The *Journal-American*, like all the other daily newspapers in New York, was suffering huge losses in advertising as a result of the still-lingering Depression and made big cuts in staff. In 1938 I, too, became unemployed. I managed to land a job with the *New York Post*, but six months later that was wiped out. That summer, after three months of unemployment, I decided to take a job at Chester's Zunbarg, the Catskills summer resort, maintaining the tennis courts and occasionally trying to teach tennis to overweight fur salesmen and Bronx schoolteachers. It was there and it was that summer that I met Helen [his first wife], who had just been divorced from a *New York Times* business page writer and was planning to spend most of her summer at Chester's.

"Helen was a very sophisticated woman—by my lights, anyway. I learned all about sex and politics from her. She was, even then, deeply involved in Communist Party politics. In fact, one year after we met, she left her Wall Street job—she was a librarian—to work as a volunteer for the Party.

"That torrid summer—emotionally, not the Catskills' fifty-degree climate—I forgot all about Pearl. At the end of the summer, I came back to Brooklyn and lived with Helen for several months before we got married. Never saw Pearl again.

"Forty years later, after coming to Providence for your commencement, I stayed for a week with Fay, now living in a posh condominium in Queens. One morning, she went shopping, and when she returned, the first thing she said was, 'Milt, you'll never guess who I ran into at the mall. You'll never guess in a million years.' I tossed out the names of some of my boyhood friends with whom I'd lost contact.

"'Believe it or not,' Fay told me, 'I ran into your old flame, Pearl. Her name's not Feinberg now. She married one of the boys from our old neighborhood who used to play tennis with us. Her name is Richman, the name of her late husband. She still looks beautiful; her hair is gray, she has two daughters and several grandchildren and lives in Queens. She gave me her phone number. I told her you were visiting from California and filled her in a little on what you were doing. She said she'd like to hear from you.'

"Well, 1978 was one year after your mother's death. I was still working my way out of my depression. And the day before, I had seen the new Neil Simon play *Act Two*, which dealt with the anguish and torment faced by the leading character, a writer, who meets a young woman shortly after his wife's death. He wrestles with the thorny problem of whether he should keep seeing this new woman in his life. He tells his brother, who encourages the relationship—'life must go on'—that he has strong guilt feelings about the new relationship because of his still passionate feelings about his late wife. The writer winds up continuing the relationship and—as the curtain falls!—marrying her. I totally rejected Neil Simon's cozy and glib ending. 'How could he marry her so soon after his wife died?' I said to myself while seated in the theater. 'What were all those professions of undying love of his deceased spouse that he made in the opening act? Just foreign propaganda? And what about those Valentine gifts he sent every year like clockwork? Phony as a three-dollar bill.' Those were the reasons I gave Fay for why I didn't feel up to calling Pearl, let alone visiting her. But the biggest reason was my shame about the shabby way I had treated her, the god-awful way I ended it. Never calling or writing. Nothing. Shameful. Unforgivable."

Superheroes

My cat, Zoomer, is exceedingly centripetal and social. The moment I spread out my papers on the dining room table, he lies on top of them. He greets most visitors by crawling onto their laps. His favorite activity is lying in front of the fire for hours while Laurie, Natalie, and I sit near him, reading. His second favorite activity is to lie between the three of us while we're watching a movie; he eats ice cream from our bowls while we pretend not to notice. At night, he sleeps in the crook of Natalie's neck, his paws wrapped around her forehead. And yet if we indulge him by petting him for too long, he inevitably reacts to this overdomestication by biting or scratching us. Zoomer loves to hide behind a bookcase and swat unsuspecting passersby or lie across the bookcase, one paw hanging in the air, and look out across the room—a lion surveying the savannah, scoping antelope. He wants to convince himself and us that, thoroughly pampered though he is, at heart he's still a killer.

From room to room he drags "his" teddy bear—what Natalie calls his girlfriend—and, despite his supposedly having been fixed years ago, dry-humps it day and night, howling with a conqueror's fury. He'll spend hours scratching the window at

his neighborhood nemesis, Fireball, but when presented with
the opportunity to confront Fireball nose-to-nose, he always
settles, pseudo-disappointedly, for the safety of imprisonment.
On the rare occasions when he does go outside, he hisses, terri-
fied, at all provocations and scoots inside on the flimsiest pre-
text. He needs to convince himself that he's a tough guy, but
really, Zoomy's a pussy.

In the movie *Spider-Man*, when Peter Parker gets bitten by a
spider and begins turning into Spider-Man, Uncle Ben tells
him, "You're changing, and that's normal. Just be careful who
you change into, okay?" Peter's change from dweeb to spider is
explicitly analogous to his transformation from boy to man.
Before he becomes Spider-Man, he wears his shirt tucked in—
dork style; afterward, he wears his undershirt and shirt hanging
out. He can't be contained. Neither can his chest, which is
newly ripped, and his eyesight is now 20/20. To Peter, his sexual maturation is the equivalent of stealing fire from the gods:
"I feel all this power, but I don't know what it means, or how to
control it, or what I'm supposed to do with it even." Teenage
boys want to believe that the sex instinct trumps and transfig-
ures the day-to-day world. One of the amazing things about
my father is that he still believed in this transfiguration deep
into his 80s.

The first time Spider-Man rescues M.J., she says to her
boyfriend, Harry, that it was "incredible." "What do you mean
'incredible'?" he keeps asking her. The second time Spider-
Man rescues M.J., she asks him, "Do I get to say thank you this
time?" and, pulling up his mask past his lips, passionately kisses
him, sending both of them into rain-drenched ecstasy. The
script makes painfully clear that Peter's newfound prowess is

procreation or, more precisely, onanism: "He wiggles his wrist, tries to get the goop to spray out, but it doesn't come." All three times Spider-Man rescues M.J., they're wrapped in a pose that looks very much like missionary sex: Spider-Man on a mission. As Peter Parker, his peter is parked; as Spider-Man, he gets to have the mythic carnival ride of sex-flight without any of the messy emotional cleanup afterward.

Spider-Man is about the concomitance of your ordinary self, which is asexual, and your Big Boy self, which is sex-driven. Virtually every male character in the film worries this division. Even the "squirrelly faced" burglar who steals the New York Wrestling Foundation's money, and who later winds up killing Ben in a car-jacking, whispers "Thanks," then flashes a sweet smile when Peter steps aside so he can get on an elevator. Ferocity and humility are in constant conversation and confusion. (Natalie: "This movie is about how everyone has a covered-up side. People don't always show you the way that they are.")

On a Saturday afternoon a few years ago, at Seattle's Green Lake pool, while I swam laps, my father swam a little, then lifted a few weights, took a sauna, and dozed, which he adamantly denied, as he always does. In the locker room, a 10-year-old kid started humming to himself, at first quite quietly, the *Batman* theme, which my father didn't recognize at first, but when I told him, he nodded. In less than a minute, the tune had made its way through the locker room—about a dozen pubescent boys humming the song. Some sang seriously; others joked around. Some stood on benches; others whapped their towels at one another's asses. Some danced around buck naked; others continued getting dressed. It was surprising and mysterious and confusing and beautiful and ridiculous and thrilling, though not to my father, who finds nearly all manifestations of mass entertainment—with the important exception of sports—appalling. "Popular culture," as he explained to me in the car on the way home, "is not real community. It's *substitute* community."

At the end of Ann Beattie's story "The Burning House," a husband and wife who are separating finally confront each other. She speaks first.

"I want to know if you're coming or going."

He takes a deep breath, lets it out, continues to lie very still.

"Everything you've done is commendable," he says. "You did the right thing to go back to school. You tried to do the right thing by finding a normal friend like Marilyn. But your whole life you've made one mistake: you've surrounded yourself with men. Let me tell you something. All men—if they're crazy, like Tucker, if they're gay as the Queen of May, like Reddy Fox, even if they're just six years old—I'm going to tell you something about them. Men think they're Spider-Man and Buck Rogers and Superman. You know what we all feel inside that you don't feel? That we're going to the stars."

He takes her hand. "I'm looking down on all this from space," he whispers. "I'm already gone."

Superman.

My father lives in Woodlake, a Bay Area condo/sports complex for senior citizens. This is a place where tough old birds come to die, but they think it's an Olympic training camp: mineral water and Frisbees. Jacuzzi, sauna, tennis courts, weight room, bingo parlor, dance hall, jet-black parking lot, jet-propelled automobiles, white stucco apartments, ice plant growing everywhere. Ducks quack across an artificial pond. Well-preserved, sun-baked septuagenarians stroll the putting green. Grandmas in string bikinis stride from the swimming pool. Dad's cohorts scamper around the courts, wearing tennis whites and floppy hats and state-of-the-art shoes and movie-star sunglasses, wielding their oversized rackets like canes and butterfly nets. My father's studio apartment is remarkable only for the sheer number of rackets, racket presses, tins of balls, shirts, shorts, sweatbands, warm-up suits, sweat socks, shoes, jocks tossed about. It isn't an apartment filled with my father. It's a pro shop filled with the sport of tennis.

In almost every piece he writes on his antique Remington for his Woodlake-sponsored writing class—a dozen women, a retired dentist, and my father meet with the teacher every other Wednesday—he projects himself as a balanced okaynik, Mr. Bonhomie. He's held more than fifty jobs in journalism and public relations and social welfare, been fired from many of them, been plagued by manic depression for fifty years, been hospitalized and received electroshock therapy countless times, is a genius at loss. Lily Tomlin was thinking of my father when she said, "Language was invented because of the deep human need to complain." He's always thrown a stone at every dog that bites, but in one story he sagely advises his friend, "You can't throw a stone at every dog that bites." My father, who may be the only person in the world with a worse sense of direction than I do, writes about another friend, "Lou can go astray in a carport. He has the worst sense of direction of any male driver in the state of California." Time after time he lets himself off way too easily. I used to want to urge him out

of this macho pose until I realized that it's a way to cheer himself up, to avoid telling mild good-bye and good-night stories,
to convince himself and us he's still a tough guy from Brooklyn
not yet ready to die.

Story after story is built on self-flattering lies: his children
from his first marriage, from whom he's estranged, didn't
attend his 95th birthday party, but now they do, bearing gifts.
He's been bald since he was 40, but now his "hair is" only
"nearly gone." My mother dies at 60 (instead of 51). Writing,
for him, is a chance to gild the lily. My dad still reads vora-
ciously and he dislikes easy sentiment in life and literature (he
recently declared J. M. Coetzee's brutal, astringent *Disgrace*
the best novel he's read in ten years), which is why his upbeat
tone fascinates and baffles.

His voice in these stories is that of a *macher*, when in reality
he's obsessed with his failures and as tough as nail polish; I
want him to write about weakness, about his weaknesses, but
instead he quotes, approvingly, a friend, who says about
women, "Remember the four F's: find 'em, feel 'em, fuck 'em,
and forget 'em." My dad, Sam Spade.

He grew up poor with four brothers and two sisters (his
mother died when he was 12 and one of his sisters died when
he was 16), but nostalgia reigns: "Ah, them were the days, the
good old days: the age of innocence, the summers of my vast
content." "I've never felt that 'at home' feeling about any other
apartment I've lived in as I did about 489 New Jersey." "Mrs.
Mason was very supportive, hugging me to her bosom at times
or drying my tears."

My father and mother divorced shortly before her death 30
years ago, and they had, by common consent, an extremely bad
relationship. But it's now a "solid-as-Gibraltar marriage." My
father, asking for time off from his boss, tells him, "I was faced

with a palace revolution and the three revolutionaries at home were getting ready to depose the king." The king he wasn't. I want him to write about forever having to polish the queen's crown according to her ever-changing and exacting specifications. I want to ask him: What did that feel like? I want to know: What is it like inside his skin? What is it like inside that bald, ill dome? Please, Dad, I want to say: only ground-level. No aerial views or airy glibness.

Hoop Dreams (iv and v)

The junior varsity played immediately after the varsity. At the end of the third quarter of the varsity game, all of us on the JV, wearing our good sweaters, good shoes, and only ties, would leave the gym to go change for our game. I loved leaving right when the varsity game was getting interesting; I loved everyone seeing us as a group, me belonging to that group, and everyone wishing us luck; I loved being part of the crowd and breaking away from the crowd to go play. And then when I was playing, I knew the crowd was there, but they slid into the distance like the overhead lights.

As a freshman I was the JV's designated shooter, our gunner whenever we faced a zone. I'd make three or four in a row, force the other team out of its zone and then sit down. I wasn't a creator. I couldn't beat anyone off the dribble, but I could shoot. Give me a step, some space, and a screen—a lot to ask for—and I was money in the bank.

Throughout my freshman and sophomore years, the JV coach told me I had to learn to take the ball to the basket and mix it up with the big guys underneath. I didn't want to, because I knew I couldn't. I already feared I was a full step slow.

The next summer I played basketball. I don't mean I got in

some games when I wasn't working at A&W or that I tried to play a couple of hours every afternoon. I mean the summer of 1972 I played basketball. Period. Nothing else. Nothing else even close to something else. All day long that summer, all summer, all night until at least eleven.

The high school court was protected by a bank of ice plant and the walls of the school. Kelly-green rims with chain nets were attached to half-moon boards that were kind only to real shooters. The court was on a grassy hill overlooking the street; when I envision Eden, I think of that court during that summer—shirts against skins, five-on-five, running the break till we keeled over. I played in pickup games, for hours alone, with friends, against friends, with people I'd never seen before and never saw again, with middle-aged men wearing college sweatshirts who liked to keep their hands on my ass as they guarded me, with friends' younger brothers who couldn't believe how good I was, with College of San Mateo players keeping in shape during the summer who told me I might make it, with coaches who told me the future of their jobs rested on my performance, with the owners of a pornographic bookstore who asked me if I wanted to appear in an art film, with my father, who asked me whatever happened to the concept of teamwork.

I played on asphalt, but also in gyms, in my mind, in rain, in winds that ruled the ball, beneath the burning sun. I wore leather weights around my ankles, taking them off only in bed, so my legs would be stronger and I'd be able to jump higher. I read every available book on technique. I jumped rope: inside, around the block, up stairs, walking the dog. Alone, I did drills outlined in an instructional book. A certain number of free throws and lay-ins from both sides and with each hand, hook shots, set shots from all over, turnaround jumpers, jumpers off the move and off the pass, tip-ins. Everything endlessly repeated. I wanted my shoulders to become as high-hung as Warriors star Rick Barry's, my wrists as taut, my glare as merciless. After a while, I'd feel like my head was the rim and my body was the ball. I was trying to put my head completely inside my body. The basketball was shot by itself. At that point I'd call it quits, keeping the feeling.

My father would tell me, "Basketball isn't just shooting. You've got to learn the rest of the game." He set up garbage cans around the court that I had to shuffle-step through, then backpedal through, then dribble through with my right hand, left hand, between my legs, behind my back. On the dead run, I had to throw the ball off a banked gutter so it came back to me as a perfect pass for a layup—the rest of the game, or so I gathered.

Mr. Rossi, the varsity coach, was wiry and quick, and most of us believed him when he alluded to his days as a floor leader at Santa Clara. He never said much. He showed a tight smile, but every now and then he'd grab you by the jersey and stand you up against a locker. Then he'd go back to smiling again.

The first few games of my junior year I started at wing for the varsity. In the first quarter against a team from Redwood City, I got the ball at the top of the key, faked left, picked up a screen right, and penetrated the lane—a rarity for me. My defender stayed with me, and when I went up for my shot we were belly-to-belly. To go forward was an offensive foul and backward was onto my butt. I tried to corkscrew around him but wasn't agile enough to change position in midair. The Redwood City guy's hip caught mine and I turned 180 degrees, landing on my leg. My left thigh tickled my right ear. I shouted curses until I passed out from the pain.

I had a broken femur and spent the winter in traction in a hospital. My doctor misread the X-rays, removing the body cast too early, so I had an aluminum pin planted next to the bone, wore a leg brace, and swung crutches all year. (I recently had the pin removed, for no particularly compelling reason of any kind other than it spooked me to think of one day being buried with a "foreign object" in my body. For one thing, it's a violation of Jewish law. Not that I'll be buried; I'll be cremated. Not that I'm religious; I'm an atheist. Still, leaving the pin in seemed to me some obscure violation of the order of things.) In the fall, the brace came off and my father tried to work with me to get back my wind and speed, but he gave up when it became obvious my heart wasn't in it. Senior year I was 10th man on a 10-man team and kept a game journal, which evolved into a sports column for the school paper. I soon realized I was better at describing basketball and analyzing it than playing it. I was pitiless on our mediocre team and the coach called me "Ace" (as in "ace reporter"), since I certainly wasn't his star ballhawk. I could shoot when left open but couldn't guard any-one quick or shake someone who hounded me tough. I fell into the role of the guy with all the answers and explanations, the well-informed benchwarmer who knew how zones were sup-posed to work but had nothing to contribute on the floor him-self. To my father's deep disappointment, I not only was not going to become a professional athlete; I was becoming, as he had been on and off throughout his life and always quite hap-pily, a sportswriter. Listen to this trip-down-memory-lane piece he wrote a few years ago for his local paper:

> Seventy-five years ago I was on the staff of the Thomas Jefferson High School newspaper, *Liberty Bell*, writing my slightly less than deathless prose about the school's athletic teams and activities. Our baseball and football teams were perpetual losers; they made a science of the

art of losing. But our basketball teams were something else; twice they won the borough championship and, in my senior year, they were in the city finals.

We played Evander Childs, a school in the Bronx, for the New York City title. The final score of that game was 27–26. That's right, 27–26. In 1928 and for a dozen more years, there was no 45-second rule when you had the ball; there was a center jump after each made field goal; and the two-handed set shot was the only shot players took.

We lost that game in the final seconds when George Gregory, Evander Childs' All-City center, slapped the ball backwards into the basket on a jump ball from eight feet away. I cursed and sobbed, by turn, for the entire hour-long subway ride home. I continued the "I-won't-or-can't-believe-what-happened" tone the next day when reporting to my buddies on the block.

Other times, other values.

I make sure to visit my father in the spring so he and I can watch the NBA playoffs together. He's a huge fan of guys who try to do it all on their own—Kobe Bryant, Allen Iverson. Solo acts. At the same time, and completely contradictorily, he tsk-tsks over every bad pass, every example of matador defense, compares every team's esprit de corps—or lack thereof—to the 1970 New York Knicks. He lives for the body in motion.

Dying Just a Little

Whereas many boys want to be superheroes who dominate the world, anorexic girls retreat from the world and sexuality. Adolescent boys are trying to become strong and aggressive, but anorexic girls are trying to become weak and fragile. Anorexia, the feminine flip side to masculine violence and heroic fantasy, comes directly from pubescent peer pressure. Teenage girls develop anorexia in specific response to sex changes. Girls become anorexic because they're trying to meet a cultural ideal of extreme thinness and/or desexualize themselves. They don't want to develop hips and breasts, and they're afraid of their bodies getting fat. The anorexic girl, wasted, tired, not menstruating, her secondary sexual characteristics slowed by poor nutrition, thus delays her entry into adulthood.

A superstition among "primitive" peoples: if a woman touches a cadaver, she'll stop menstruating.

Ninety percent of anorexics are female. Seventy percent of women say that looking at models in fashion magazines causes them to feel depressed, guilty, and shameful. Ninety-five percent of people who enroll in formal weight-reduction programs are women. Ninety-eight percent of women gain back the weight they lose by dieting. Women regard themselves as fat if they're 15 pounds overweight; men don't think of themselves as fat unless they're 35 pounds above the U.S. average. My father has always been girlishly proud of his quite thin waist; the first thing he comments upon whenever he sees me is whether I've lost or gained weight. His most rapturous praise: "You're slender as a reed." Eighty percent of people who have part of their small intestines removed in order to help themselves lose weight are women. Fifty-five percent of adolescent girls believe they're overweight; only 13 percent of adolescent girls are actually overweight. Anorexia has the highest fatality rate of any psychiatric illness. Eleven percent of Americans would abort a fetus if they were told it had a tendency toward obesity. When asked to identify good-looking individuals, 5-year-olds invariably select pictures of thin people. Elementary school children have more negative attitudes toward the obese than toward bullies, the disabled, or children of another race. Teachers routinely underestimate the intelligence of fat kids and overestimate the intelligence of slender kids. Corpulent students are less likely to be granted scholarships. Anorexics often grow lanugo, which is soft, woolly body hair that grows to compensate for the loss of fat cells so the body can hold in heat. Anorexics have many of the physical symptoms of starvation: their bellies are distended, their hair is dull and brittle, their periods stop, they're weak, and they're vulnerable to infections. They also have the psychological characteristics of the starving: they're depressed, irritable, pessimistic, apathetic, and preoccupied with food. They dream of feasts.

·   ·   ·

Girls and women quoted in Kim Chernin's *The Obsession: Reflections on the Tyranny of Slenderness*:

"I've heard about that illness, anorexia nervosa, and I keep looking around for someone who has it. I want to go sit next to her. I think to myself, maybe I'll catch it."

"One of my cousins used to throw food under the table when no one was looking. Finally, she got so thin they had to take her to the hospital. I always admired her."

"I'm embarrassed to have bulimia. It's such a preppy disease."

"I don't care how long it takes. One day I'm going to get my body to obey me. I'm going to make it lean and tight and hard. I'll succeed in this, even if it kills me."

"To have control over your body becomes an extreme accomplishment. You make of your body your very own kingdom where you are the tyrant, the absolute dictator."

"Look, see how thin I am, even thinner than you wanted me to be. You can't make me eat more. I am in control of my fate, even if my fate is starving."

"I get lots of compliments. My friends are jealous, but I've made new friends. Guys who never considered me before have been asking me out."

"I hate to say this, but I'd rather binge than make out."

"In all the years I've been a therapist, I've yet to meet one girl who likes her body."

I was in my mid-20s. Before taking off her clothes, she said she needed to tell me something: she had herpes. Madly in love with her witchy bitchiness, I found occasional enforced celibacy insanely erotic, the way a chastity belt glamorizes what it locks out. We wound up living together, and as we fell out of love with each other, her herpes became a debate point between us. She suggested that we just get married and then if I got it, I got it, and who would care? I suggested she at least explore some of the possibilities of which modern medicine availed us.

For a multitude of reasons, the two of us didn't belong together, but what interests me now is what, for lack of a better term, a free-floating signifier the virus was. When I was in love with her, it eroticized her. When I wasn't, it repelled me. The body has no meanings. We bring meanings to it.

As psychologist Nancy Etcoff says, in *Survival of the Prettiest*, "In a context where only a king can control enough food resources and labor supply to eat enough and do no physical labor so that he becomes fat, prestige is conferred by signs of abundance. A thin person is a person too poor to afford the calories, and maybe one who does so much physical labor that she cannot keep weight on. When poor women are fat (because junk food is so cheap and available, and they are less educated about its hazards and unable to afford expensive healthy foods), then it's in to be thin and dietary restraint and physical exercise become prestigious."

"I can't stand fat women," a thin woman says in *The Obsession*. "If one of them has been sitting on a chair in a coffee shop, or on the bus, and there's no other place to sit, I won't go in there or sit in that place."

"It's like watching a death's head," another woman says about a fat woman at the market. "The co-op ought to pay her to get out of here. Who can go home to a good dinner with that in mind?"

My father's term of derision for big-bellied men: "water-melon smugglers."

Laurie and I stage monthly dieting competitions, though neither of us is overweight. "Want a second helping?" "I made some banana bread for you." What's going on here? We're each saying: you're beautiful; I, though, am wanting; I will do anything for love.

Fasting frees one from carnal needs and desires, prepares one for visions and trances. Moses fasted 40 days before receiving the Ten Commandments. Jesus fasted 40 days before his enlightenment. Medieval saints (especially women) fasted to demonstrate their purity and holiness, and if their fasting appeared to continue far beyond normal human bounds, it was proof of God's grace. By controlling their breathing, nuns in ancient times were able to stop menstruating and limit their need for food.

Fasting is a constant for female saints. In the thirteenth century, Margaret of Cortona said, "I want to die of starvation to satiate the poor." Thérèse of Lisieux died of tuberculosis in 1897, just short of her 25th birthday. As she lay dying, bleeding from her intestines and unable to keep down water, she was tormented by the thought of banquets. Gemma Galgani died in 1903—also of TB, also at 25. She dreamed of food; would it be all right, she asked her confessor, to ask Jesus to take away her sense of taste? Permission was granted. She arranged with Jesus that she should begin to expiate, through her own suffering, all the sins committed by priests. For the next 60 days she vomited whenever she tried to eat.

In 1859, an American doctor, William Stout Chipley, published an article describing a condition he called "sitophobia,"

fear of food. In 1868, William Withey Gull, the English physician who was suspected of being Jack the Ripper, first mentioned anorexia nervosa; in 1873, he delivered a lecture on the
disorder. The same year, a French doctor, Charles-Ernest
Lasègue, published a long article on what he called "hysterical
anorexia." Lasègue described the following symptoms: menstruation ceases, thirst increases, the abdomen retracts and
loses elasticity, constipation becomes obstinate, the skin is pale
and dry, the pulse is quickened, the patient tires easily, and
when she rises from resting often experiences vertigo—all of
which are still associated with anorexia.

In the late nineteenth century, a tepid appetite was proof of
a woman's delicacy and elegance. A young lady who admitted
to a hearty appetite would be said to "eat like a ploughboy" and
would be the object of sneers and jests. Victorian women, even
when they became mothers, were admonished never to demonstrate their hunger. If they did confess to hunger, they were
expected to yearn only for light, sweet, delicate morsels and
not for meat, which was thought to stimulate sexual desire. For
a woman to enjoy a slab of roast beef was to suggest a baser
nature that she was not supposed to acknowledge in herself.

In 2004, Hilary Mantel wrote, "Why do women still feel so
hounded? The ideal body seems now attainable only by plastic
surgery. The ideal woman has the earning powers of a chief
executive, breasts like an inflatable doll, no hips at all, and the
tidy, hairless labia of an unviolated 6-year-old. The world gets
harder and harder. There's no pleasing it. No wonder some
girls want out. Anorexia itself seems like mad behaviour, but I
don't think it is madness. It is a way of shrinking back, of
reserving, preserving the self, fighting free of sexual and emotional entanglements. It says, like Christ, *noli me tangere*.
Touch me not and take yourself off. For a year or two, it may

be a valid strategy; to be greensick, to be out of the game; to die just a little; to nourish the inner being while starving the outer being; to buy time. Most anorexics do recover, after all. Anorexia can be an accommodation, a strategy for survival."

In *Cymbeline*, Imogen apparently dies when she's about 15. Her brothers, Guiderius and Arviragus, stand over her grave and chant a dirge over what they think is her lifeless body inside her coffin: "Golden lads and girls all must / As chimney-sweepers, come to dust." Then Imogen opens her eyes and comes back to life.

Ye Olde Mind-Body Problem

In accordance with the Federal Cigarette Labeling and
Advertising Act, all advertisements for tobacco products
in the United States must include one of these four
Surgeon General's warning labels:

SURGEON GENERAL'S WARNING: Smoking Causes
  Lung Cancer, Heart Disease, Emphysema, and May
  Complicate Pregnancy.
SURGEON GENERAL'S WARNING: Quitting
  Smoking Now Greatly Reduces Serious Risks to Your
  Health.
SURGEON GENERAL'S WARNING: Cigarette Smoke
  Contains Carbon Monoxide.
SURGEON GENERAL'S WARNING: Smoking by
  Pregnant Women May Result in Fetal Injury,
  Premature Birth, and Low Birth Weight.

All four warnings must be used with equal frequency, but
tobacco companies can choose when to use each warning.
In compliance with the Federal Cigarette Labeling and
Advertising Act, advertisements feature each of the four

Surgeon General's warnings with the same frequency—about 25 percent each. However, in the study sample of 52 ads in eighteen magazines, the warning to pregnant women occurs far more often in the ads in men's magazines (*Sports Illustrated, Esquire, GQ*), 53 percent of the time, while this same warning occurs in only 20 percent of the ads in women's magazines (*Mademoiselle, McCall's, Ms., Vogue, Working Woman*).

The warning that cigarette smoke contains carbon monoxide occurs in 37 percent of the ads in women's magazines but occurs in none of the ads in men's magazines. The advertisements featuring the carbon monoxide warning usually feature youthful, carefree, and less serious-appearing women. Carbon monoxide is a poisonous gas that interferes with the body's oxygen-carrying mechanisms; advertisers apparently assume that women, especially young women, are less apt than men to know this fact.

The magazine with the most cigarette advertisements, *Mademoiselle*, has a young, female audience. Eighty-eight percent of smokers start before age 20, and the only group that smokes more now than it did 20 years ago is adolescent girls.

Tobacco companies appear to manipulate the use of the Surgeon General's warning to render them as ineffective as possible, mitigating the purpose of the warning by often using the warning they presume the reader is most likely to ignore.

Whenever I reread this précis for a poli sci paper Laurie wrote eons ago, I never fail to be moved by her belief/hope that the actions human beings take might be based to any degree whatsoever on rational thought. All the evidence points to the fact that they're not (cf. anorexia). My father being, of course, the exception: he took up pipe smoking in the early '50s (in photo-album pictures from that period he looks improbably dignified), but he gave it up immediately after realizing, during a tennis match, that it was cutting down on his wind.

Sex and Death (ii)

In many insect species, when the female emerges from her sac as a mature life form, males immediately swarm around her, fighting desperately to mate with her. She mates, then dies after laying her eggs. Instead of the juvenile stages being preliminary to the fully formed adult life form, the adult life form exists only as the culmination of the juvenile life form, as a way for the cycle to continue.

In animals that produce all their offspring at once, like the salmon, most of the life span is spent getting ready for reproduction. The animal grows, stores energy, and prepares its gonads for one explosion. When the hormonal signal is given, resources are mobilized to maximize reproductive effort, even if this leaves the animal so damaged and depleted that it dies soon after. A salmon's life span is significantly extended if it's castrated before its gonads develop.

As the August mating season nears for the male marsupial mouse, its testosterone levels build steadily higher, reaching a peak in late July. The adrenal glands enlarge, sending elevated levels of hormones into the bloodstream. Males enter a state of extreme physiological excitement and stress. They engage in violent battles with one another for the opportunity to mate with the females. After mating, the males have—in addition to the scars from the battle—stomach ulcers that bleed severely. Their immune systems are so decimated that they easily fall prey to parasites. Nearly all of them will die in the course of the next few days. The females survive to raise and suckle their fatherless young, but they, too, are extremely fragile. Only a few females survive to breed again the following year.

A boy's first ejaculations are nocturnal emissions: uncontrolled and unprompted acts. A boy's body mechanically begins the process of sexual reproduction without much if any input on his part. And it's fundamentally similar with girls (granting obvious, important differences). Before you are even really used to being alive and moving around in the world, much less have any understanding of yourself, your body's already starting the reproductive process.

For most of human history, people mated as teenagers and conceived their first child by age 20. When anthropologist Suzanne Frayser studied 454 traditional cultures, she found that the average age for brides was 12 to 15; for grooms, 18.

In the last 30 years, the suicide rate has doubled among American children and adolescents; it's the third leading cause of death in youth. The tumult of hormones is, for some teenagers, too much: a hugely disproportionate number of school shootings occur in spring.

Hoop dream (vi):

My junior year of high school, a month before I broke my leg, while we dressed for our first league game, our coach, Mr. Rossi, stood at the blackboard in the locker room, shaking and crumbling chalk. At first we thought he was just trying to get us psyched up. He stubbed his toe on the bench. We got on our road uniforms and tube socks and assumed maybe Mr. Rossi had had a taste or two too many. Then he burst out with it.

"Dicky Schroeder," he said. And we all realized: where the hell was Dicky, home with a head cold when we had Lincoln at Lincoln? Give him a couple of aspirin and send him over there in a cab, right, Mr. Rossi?

"Dicky had a bad accident in his garage last night. His parents said it wasn't an accident. Dicky's not with us any longer."

We closed our lockers. It took us a while to grasp what Mr. Rossi said, and it took us the rest of the year for it to sink in. Dicky Schroeder smoked Raleighs and drove a souped-up Chevy. He was always buying new clothes and car accessories and bullshitting you about getting laid. He was too busy to kill himself.

Around a week later, the school paper ran an obituary, quoting people saying what a solid student he'd been, which was an insult to everyone's intelligence. The article finished up with a quote from Ralph Waldo Emerson saying, "Death isn't an ending; it's only a transition," which did everyone a lot of good, knowing Dicky wasn't gone forever: he was just running the transition game.

Immediately after Mr. Rossi told us Dicky had committed suicide, he asked us if we wanted to play the game and, to his surprise and perhaps our own, we all said yes. No one talked on the bus to the game and none of us took warm-ups. Once the game started, we all tried to play like Dicky, looking to pass, working the give-and-go. Everyone was looking for the open man, and the open man was Dicky. We were all hoping to wake up and find out he was only kidding. If we all tried to play like him, maybe he'd pop out from under his garage door and show us how to run the three-on-two. The play I'll remember until I'm 90 was Brad Gamble, our star, all alone on a breakaway, me trailing. He stopped and set the ball down on the floor for me to pick up. I looked for someone to follow after me; I kept waiting, but no one came. I banked it off the board, and we won in a romp.

Adulthood and
Middle Age

Decline and Fall (ii)

If you could live forever in good health at a particular age, what age would you be? As people get older, their ideal age gets higher. For 18- to 24-year-olds, it's age 27; for 25- to 29-year-olds, it's 31; for 30- to 39-year-olds, it's 37; for 40- to 49-year-olds, it's 40; for 50- to 64-year-olds, it's 44; and for people over 64, it's 59.

Your IQ is highest between ages 18 and 25. Once your brain peaks in size—at age 25—it starts shrinking, losing weight, and filling with fluid. In a letter to his father, Carlyle wrote that his brother, Jack, "decides, as a worthy fellow of twenty always will decide, that mere external rank and convenience are nothing; the dignity of mind is all in all. I argue, as every reasonable man of twenty-eight, that this is poetry in part, which a few years will mix pretty largely with prose." Goethe said, "Whoever is not famous at twenty-eight must give up any dreams of glory."

When I was 31, I was informed that someone had written, in a stall in the women's bathroom in a bookstore, "David Shields is a great writer and a babe to boot." This is pretty much the high point of my life, when my acne was long gone and I still had hair and was thin without dieting and could still wear contacts and thought I was going to become famous. (Just recently, looking for compliments, I asked my father what he thought of what I've become, and he said, "You were such a great athlete as a kid. I thought sure you were going to be a pro basketball player or baseball player.") Sir William Osler said, "The effective, moving, vitalizing work of the world is done between the ages of twenty-five and forty." Which is in fact true: creativity peaks in the 30s, then declines rapidly; most creative achievements occur when people are in their 30s. Degas said, "Everyone has talent at twenty-five; the difficulty is to have it at fifty." The consolation of the library: when you're 45, your vocabulary is three times as large as it is at 20. When you're 60, your brain possesses four times the information that it does at 20.

Your strength and coordination peak at 19. Your body is the most flexible until age 20; after that, joint function steadily declines. World-class sprinters are almost always in their late teens or early 20s. Your stamina peaks in your late 20s or early 30s; marathon records are invariably held by 25- to 35-year-olds.

When you're young, your lungs have a huge reserve capacity; even world-class athletes rarely push their lungs to the limit. But as you age, your lungs get less elastic: you can't fill them as full or empty them as completely of stale air. Aerobic capacity decreases 1 percent per year between ages 20 and 60.

"It isn't sex that causes trouble for young ballplayers," Casey Stengel said. "It's staying up all night looking for it."

"During the summers of 1938 and '39," my father wrote in a piece for his class, "I worked as a keeper of the tennis courts and occasionally as tennis instructor at Chester's Zunbarg—

Sun Hill—a small, 120-capacity resort in the Catskills Mountains 80 miles northeast of New York City. The first day of that first summer, Anne Chester briefed me on the job I was about to step into at her hotel: 'The salary is small—just $200 for the summer—and I apologize for it, but the fringe benefits more than make up for it.'

"What fringe benefits?" I asked in my youthful ignorance.

"It won't take long for you to find out what they are," she said, with a sly wink.

Twenty-four hours later, a sultry brunette walked up to me on the courts and asked if I gave tennis lessons.

I said I did and asked her what day and time would be convenient for her lesson.

"And do you give any other lessons besides tennis?" trilled this siren-cum-tennis pupil.

"Just tennis, lady," I managed to squeeze out, extending my hand. "The name's Milt and I'll see you here tomorrow at 10."

"Yes, I know," she replied, still holding my hand. "I'll be there." I thought she'd never let go. I needed that right hand for serving up the ball. "The name's Eva, Eva Gordon."

The next morning, at a few minutes before 10, I was on the courts with a bushel of used tennis balls and a galloping curiosity as to what kind of tennis player this hand-holding Jezebel would turn out to be. 10:15 and no Eva. Was it all a none-too-subtle ploy to meet and size up the new tennis pro? Conventional wisdom has it that tennis teachers are glamorous and sexy guys, though you wouldn't recognize me from that description.

Just when I was ready to give up on her, Eva strolled leisurely onto the court, saying, "Here I am, Coach." She was dressed to the nines in flaming red shorts and a low-cut halter that showed her heart was in the right place.

"Let's get started," I snapped, very businesslike. I had another guest coming for a lesson at 11.

Eva was a revelation on the courts. She had the smoothest forehand this side of Helen Wills and a backhand that tore the cover off the ball.

"Do you play for some school?" I asked, signaling a brief time out.

"Yes, Hunter College in the city," she replied.

Eva stayed for two weeks at Chester's that first time and took a lesson every day. We also played quite a few sets—ahem—off the courts. She was just as good and explosive at that extracurricular activity as she was on the court.

She returned twice more during the summer for week-long stays and—er—lessons. By Labor Day, we were damned serious, but I had to get back to the city and try to find a job in the heart of the Depression and Eva had to complete her education at Hunter. What's more, we both knew (we weren't moonstruck kids) that we'd had a summer fling, one to be treasured, but—for a lot of reasons—not followed up. It was great while it lasted, we both agreed over a tall drink at the hotel bar.

Arteriosclerosis can begin as early as age 20.

As you age, your responses to stimuli of all kinds become slower and more inaccurate, especially in more complex tasks. From age 20 to 60, your reaction time to noise slows 20 percent. At 60, you make more errors in verbal learning tasks. At 70, you will experience a decline in your ability to detect small changes, such as the movement of a clock hand.

Given a list of 24 words, an average 20-year-old remembers 14 of the words, a 40-year-old remembers 11, a 60-year-old remembers 9, and a 70-year-old remembers 7.

Most people reach skeletal maturity by their early 20s. At 30, you reach peak bone mass. Your bones are as dense and strong as they'll ever be. Human bones, with their astonishing blend of strength and flexibility, can withstand pressure of about 24,000 pounds per square inch—four times that of reinforced concrete—but if you were to remove the mineral deposits, what you would have left would be flexible enough to tie into knots. In your late 30s, you start losing more bone than you make. At first you lose bone slowly, 1 percent a year. The older you get, the more you lose.

Beginning in your early 20s, your ability to detect salty or bitter things decreases, as does your ability to identify odors. The amount of ptyalin, an enzyme used to digest starches, in your saliva decreases after age 20. After age 30, your digestive tract displays a decrease in the amount of digestive juices. At 20, in other words, your fluids are fleeing, and by 30, you're drying up.

Lauren Bacall said, "When a woman reaches twenty-six in America, she's on the slide. It's downhill all the way from then on. It doesn't give you a tremendous feeling of confidence and well-being."

Jimi Hendrix died at age 27, as did Janis Joplin, Jim Morrison, Brian Jones of the Stones, Kurt Cobain, and bluesman Robert Johnson.

Until you're 30, your grip strength increases; after 40, it declines precipitously. After age 65, your lower arm and back muscle strength declines. Owing to reduced coordination rather than loss of strength, your power output—e.g., your ability to turn a crank over a period of time—falls after age 50. My father, on the other hand, could defeat me in arm-wrestling halfway into his 60s.

At age 30, men show a decline in enthusiasm for typically masculine activities such as sports, drinking, and car repairs. Be grateful, I say, for small favors. Still, easily one of the happiest moments of my life occurred when, nearly 30 and in grad school, I went with several of my classmates to the gym to play basketball. Out on the wing on a fast break, I caught the ball, reverse-spun on William Mayfield, who started at forward for the University of Iowa basketball team, and beat him to the hoop. (Was he dogging it? Who knows? I don't want to know.) My fellow grad-student nerds went nuts; they all kept saying, "You don't even look like a basketball player!" Glasses, love handles, etc. Hoop dream (vii), undoubtedly.

Nicholas Murray said, "Many people's tombstones should read, 'Died at 30. Buried at 60.'" The ancient Persians believed that the first 30 years should be spent living life and the last 40 years should be spent understanding it. Reversing the time periods, Schopenhauer said, "The first forty years of life give us the text; the remaining thirty provide the commentary on it." According to Rousseau: "Man is always the same: at ten he is led by sweetmeats; at twenty by a mistress; at thirty by pleasure; at forty by ambition; at fifty by avarice; after that, what is left for him to run after but wisdom?" At every age, 10 or 90, my father has been a pleasure-seeking missile.

Since your vertebral column continues to grow until you're 30, you might gain anywhere from three to five millimeters in height between ages 20 and 30. Starting at 30, though, you lose one-sixteenth of an inch in height per year; your posture changes because your vertebrae shrink while your hips and knees bend closer to the ground and your foot arch flattens. My father has shrunk from 5'10" to 5'7". As you age, your body loses water and your organs shrink: your body consumes 12 fewer calories per day for each year of age over 30.

For most people, the ability to hear higher sound frequencies begins to decline in their 30s; men are 3½ times more likely than women to show a decline in their ability to hear high notes. Whatever level of loss is found, it will get, on average, 2½ times worse each decade. The sweat glands that keep the auditory canal moist die off one by one; ear wax becomes drier and crustier, and hard wax builds up to block out sounds. One-third of hearing loss in older people is due to this buildup. Your eardrum becomes thinner and more flaccid, causing the drum to be less easily vibrated by sound waves. You progressively lose your ability to hear sound at all frequencies.

The limbic system—"the seat of emotions"—exists in a part of the brain, the hippocampus, that humans share with lizards. (Your brain has three layers: the brain stem, controlling basic functions and basic emotions, is the reptilian layer; the mammalian layer houses more complex mental functions such as learning and adaptability; and the third layer constitutes most of the human brain—the cerebral cortex and cerebellum—which allows us to use language and perform complex acts of memory.) Beginning at age 30, parts of the hippocampus die off.

Emerson said, "After thirty, a man wakes up sad every morning, excepting perhaps five or six, until the day of his death."

At 31, Tolstoy said, "At our age, when you have reached, not merely by the process of thought but with your whole being and your whole life, an awareness of the uselessness and impossibility of seeking enjoyment; when you feel that what seemed like torture has become the only substance of life—work and toil—then searchings, anguish, dissatisfaction with yourself, remorse, etc.—the attributes of youth—are inappropriate and useless."

Before being guillotined, Camille Desmoulins, one of the leaders of the French Revolution, when asked how old he was (he was 34), said, "I am 33—the age of the good sans-culotte Jesus, an age fatal to revolutionists."

By age 35, nearly everyone shows some of the signs of aging, such as graying hair, wrinkles, less strength, less speed, stiffening in the walls of the central arteries, degeneration of the heart's blood vessels, diminished blood supply to the brain, elevated blood pressure. In my father's case, the only sign of aging at 35 was a rapidly receding hairline. One out of three American adults has high blood pressure. The maximum rate your heart can attain is your age subtracted from 220 and therefore falls by one beat every year. Your heart is continually becoming a less efficient pumping machine.

You couldn't prove this decline in efficiency by my dad, who, until his early 90s, would awake in darkness in order to lace up his sneakers and tug on his jogging suit. Birds would be just starting to call; black would still streak the colored-pencil soft blue of the sky: my father would be jogging. In an hour, he'd run 20 (then, when he got older, 15 and, later, 10) times around a track that was without bleachers or lighting or lanes, that had weeds in the center and a dry water fountain at the end of the far straightaway and a running path littered with glass and rocks. He didn't care. He pounded his feet through the dirt and pumped his arms and kept his rubbery legs moving until, by the very stomping of his feet, night withdrew and morning came. As he once wrote me, apropos of nothing in particular, "I am, no surprise, that same skinny kid who ran with the speed of Pegasus through Brownsville's streets in quest of a baseball."

Rheumatoid arthritis most frequently begins between ages 35 and 55.

In 1907, the French writer Paul Léautaud, at 36, said, "I was asked the other day, 'What are you doing nowadays?' 'I'm busy growing older,' I answered."

In *My Dinner with André*, Wallace Shawn says, "I grew up on the Upper East Side, and when I was ten years old I was rich, an aristocrat, riding around in taxis, surrounded by comfort, and all I thought about was art and music. Now I'm thirty-six, and all I think about is money."

Mozart died at 35; Byron, at 36; Raphael and Van Gogh, at 37.

James Boswell, Samuel Johnson's biographer, said, "I must fairly acknowledge that in my opinion the disagreement between young men and old is owing rather to the fault of the latter than of the former. Young men, though keen and impetuous, are usually very well disposed to receive the counsels of the old, if they are treated with gentleness, but old men forget in a wonderful degree their own feelings in the early part of life." When Boswell wrote this, he was 37 and Samuel Johnson was 69. Whenever I mention an accomplishment of mine to my father, he quickly changes the subject or mentions a more impressive accomplishment by someone else. I asked him once whether, in his view, competition was built into any relationship between father and son, and he briskly denied it, saying he's never felt anything except pride and admiration.

Former London Symphony Orchestra conductor Colin Davis said, at 38, "I think that to so many what happens is the death of ambition in the conventional sense. That great driving motor that prods you and exasperates you and brings out the worst qualities in you for about twenty years is beginning to be a bit moth-eaten and tired. I find that I'm altogether much quieter, I think. I don't love music any less, but there's not the excess of energy I used to spend in enthusiasm and in intoxication. I feel much freer than I've ever been in my life."

The oldest person ever to play in the NBA was 43. The oldest person ever to hold a boxing title was 45. The oldest age at which anyone broke a track-and-field record was 41, in 1909. The oldest person to win an Olympic gold medal was 42, in 1920. In the prologue to *The Canterbury Tales*, Chaucer wrote, "If gold ruste, what shal iren do?"

At age 40, your preference for fast-paced activity declines.

Beginning at 40, your white blood cells, which fight cancer and infectious diseases, have a lowered capacity.

Jack London died at 40; Elvis Presley, at 42.

On my 30th birthday, under my girlfriend's influence, I got my left ear pierced and bought a diamond earring. I wore various earrings over the next 10 years or so, but wearing an earring never really worked for me. Earrings forced me to confront the nature of my style, or lack of style. I'm certainly not macho enough to wear an earring as if I were a tough guy, but neither am I effeminate enough to wear an earring in my right ear as if I were maybe gay-in-training. Instead, I'm just muddling through, and the earring forced me, over time, to see this, acknowledge it, and respond to it. On my 40th birthday, under the influence of Natalie, who thought it made me look like a pirate, I took out the earring I was then wearing—a gold hoop—and haven't worn an earring since.

F. Scott Fitzgerald, who died at 44, wrote in his notebook, "Drunk at 20, wrecked at 30, dead at 40."

Each year, more fat gets deposited in the walls of medium and larger arteries, causing the arterial walls to narrow. The weight of your small intestine decreases; the volume and weight of your kidneys shrink. Total blood flow to the kidney decreases by 10 percent for every decade after the age of 40. Every organ will eventually get less nourishment than it needs to do its job.

Don Marquis, an American newspaper columnist who died at 59, said, "Forty and forty-five are bad enough; fifty is simply hell to face; fifteen minutes after that you are sixty; and then in ten minutes more you are eighty-five."

"Forty-five," said Joseph Conrad, "is the age of recklessness for many men, as if in defiance of the decay and death waiting with open arms in the sinister valley at the bottom of the inevitable hill." Those clichés of male midlife crisis—having an affair, for instance, or buying a red sports car—are, on a biological level, anyway, profound rebellions of the "rage, rage, against the dying of the light" sort. My father's first marriage broke apart when he had an affair with a gorgeous, red-haired editor at the *Los Angeles Herald Express*, one picture of whom appeared—somewhat bizarrely—in our family photo album.

Cicero said, "Old age begins at forty-six." He died at 53.

John Kennedy died at 46.

Virginia Woolf said, "Control of life is what one should learn now: its economic management. I feel cautious, like a poor person, now I am forty-six."

Victor Hugo said, "Forty is the old age of youth. Fifty is the youth of old age."

On my 10th birthday, when my father was 56, he pitched so hard to me and my friends that we were afraid to hit against him. "Get in the batter's box," he growled at us.

Bloodline to Star Power (ii)

In 1955, my parents were living in Los Angeles, my mother was working for the ACLU, and she asked my father to ask Joseph Schildkraut to participate in an ACLU-sponsored memorial to Albert Einstein, who had died in April. "After all," my father wrote in reply to one of my innumerable requests for more information, "Einstein was a German Jew and Pepi [Schildkraut's nickname] had spent so much of his professional life in Berlin and was a member of a group of prominent people who had fled Germany in the years before Hitler and lived in the Pacific Palisades–Santa Monica area."

My father got Schildkraut's phone number and called him, telling him he was a Schildkraut, too, and inviting him to speak at the memorial tribute. "After much backing-and-filling and long, pregnant pauses (his, not mine) on the phone," my father said, Schildkraut told my father to bring him the script. A few days later my father went to Schildkraut's house in Beverly Hills to show him the script he would read at the memorial if he decided to appear on the program. Schildkraut came to the door, greeting Shields (né Shildcrout) stiffly. "He was very businesslike—cold, distant." For a moment or two they talked about their families. My father told him about the backstage visit in 1923. Joseph knew absolutely nothing of the Schild-kraut family's ancestry. "Joseph Schildkraut, I would say," my father said, "and I think it's a fair statement, was somebody who didn't think about his Jewish heritage."

Schildkraut talked to my father for about thirty minutes in the foyer of the big, rambling house. "Later, in telling the story, I often exaggerated—said he clicked his heels, Prussian-like. He really didn't." Schildkraut said that he had to show the script to Dore Schary for approval. (Schary was a writer who had become the head of production at RKO and then MGM. Anti-Communist fears lingered; the blacklist was still in effect.) Schildkraut told Shields to come back in a week.

When my father returned, Schildkraut again talked with him rapidly in the foyer of the house—"On neither visit did he have me come into the living room, nor did he introduce me to his wife, who was moving about in the next room"—and wound up saying that Schary had read the script and said it was all right. The script was taken almost entirely from Einstein's writings on civil liberties, academic freedom, and freedom of speech. The memorial was held at what was then the Holly-wood Athletic Club and later became the University of Judaism. Also on the platform were Linus Pauling; A. L. Wirin, the chief counsel to the ACLU; John Howard Lawson, a screenwriter and the unofficial spokesman for the "Holly-wood Ten"; Anne Revere, who before being blacklisted won an Academy Award as best supporting actress for her performance as Elizabeth Taylor's mother in *National Velvet*; and a novelist who my father insists was once famous and who in any case has a name worthy of the Marx Brothers—Lion Feuchtwanger.

The event was free. Every seat in the immense auditorium was filled. Hundreds of people sat in the aisles. Eason Monroe, the executive director of the ACLU and a man upon whom my mother had an immense, lifelong crush, asked the overflow audience to find seats or standing room in several small rooms upstairs. Monroe assured them that all the speakers would come upstairs to address them after speaking in the main auditorium. The program started a little late, about 8:30 P.M., but Schildkraut still hadn't shown up. Monroe asked Shields, "Milt, where's your cousin? It's getting late." My father assured Monroe he'd be there. "He was too big a ham to stay away on such an occasion." His name had appeared prominently in the ads as one of the main speakers.

Finally, Schildkraut showed. Monroe greeted him and asked him if, as the others had consented to do, he would also speak to the groups upstairs. Schildkraut said that first he'd speak to the main auditorium audience; then he'd "see."

The other speakers—Pauling, Wirin, Lawson, Revere, and Feuchtwanger—spoke to the audience in the main auditorium, were "warmly received" (whatever that means), then went upstairs to speak once again to the overflow audience in a couple of anterooms. "The occasion lifted even the most uninspired speaker and material to emotional heights," according to my father. "But then came Pepi, the last speaker on the program. When he got to the podium, the audience was noisy and restless. After all, people were feeling the emotion of the memorial to this great man. Schildkraut took one look out there and employed the actor's stratagem: he whispered the first line or two, and a hush fell over the audience. Then, when he was sure he had their attention, he thundered the next lines. When he finished, he got a standing ovation. And this for a political naïf, or worse: a man who certainly didn't agree with everything he had just read, or anything else Einstein stood for. But he was the consummate actor, and he read his lines— to perfection."

When Schildkraut finished, my father asked him about going upstairs. Schildkraut looked right through Shields and walked out the door. "Now he truly was like a Prussian soldier. That's the last time I saw him. In person, that is. Of course, I saw *The Diary of Anne Frank* on the screen half a dozen times. And if it's ever on television, I watch it again."

Boys vs. Girls (iii)

By ages 30 to 34, women are 85 percent as fertile as they were at 20 to 24, and the rate declines to 35 percent by 40 to 44, and to virtually 0 percent after age 50. Among men, the decline in fertility is more gradual: at 45 to 50, men retain 90 percent of their peak fertility, a rate that declines to only 80 percent after 55. Males who mate with older women pass on less genetic coding, while females can mate with older men without the same problem.

On January 22, 2005, in Palm Beach, Florida, at Bethesda-by-the-Sea Episcopal Church, before 400 of their friends, Donald Trump, now 61, who is estimated to be worth $2.5 billion, married his companion of six years, blue-eyed Slovenian-Austrian model Melania Knauss, now 37. Trump was previously married to models Marla Maples and Ivana Winklmayr. Two sons and a daughter from his first marriage, and his daughter from his second marriage, attended the half-hour wedding, which was the culmination of three days of celebrations.

At the ceremony, the bride, who said she may want to have children (when her baby was born the following year, the baby pictures were sold to *People* for what were estimated to be "the mid-six figures"), lit the unity candle that she had used during her baptism. Knauss said she wanted an event that was "chic, elegant, simple, and sexy." Her dress was made of 300 feet of white satin, had a 13-foot train, weighed 50 pounds, took all 28 of Christian Dior's seamstresses 1,000 hours to stitch, and took an additional 50 hours to embroider. Trump said about Knauss, "When we walk into a restaurant, I watch grown men weep."

According to French chef Jean-Georges Vongerichten, who donated his services, the new Mrs. Trump has "impeccable taste"; Donald Trump is his landlord. The wedding cake stood two yards high and was covered with 3,000 sugar roses. The reception, held at Trump's Mar-a-Lago mansion, featured a 36-piece orchestra.

Billy Joel, who at 55 had recently married "restaurant correspondent" Katie Lee, 23, in a wedding at which his daughter, Alexa Ray, 19, was a maid of honor, said Trump's wedding was a "beautiful ceremony."

When he was 53, John Derek was asked by Barbara Walters whether he would still love his wife, Bo Derek, then 23, if she were disfigured or paralyzed. He thought for a moment and said no. Bo Derek tried hard to smile, but she couldn't.

Sex Changes (Everything)

Menopause, which typically occurs between ages 45 and 50, is unique to humans, for which there's a good evolutionary reason: by age 50, a mother is beginning to experience many of the adverse effects of aging. She enhances her genetic contribution to future generations if she stops having babies of her own and thereby increases the likelihood that she'll survive to raise her children and assist with her grandchildren.

Menopause happens gradually: 10 or more years before they cease menstruation, women may experience briefer cycles. At age 30, women typically get their periods every 28 to 30 days; at age 40, every 25 days; at 46, every 23 days. After age 35, women's eggs are more genetically defective; if fertilization occurs, the babies produced are more likely to have birth defects. The follicles stop obeying orders from the brain to make estrogen. The amount of estrogen, especially estradiol, the most powerful estrogen, becomes scarce.

As women lose estrogen, their pubic hair becomes more sparse, the labia become more wrinkled, and the skin surrounding the vulva atrophies. The cell walls of a woman's vagina become weaker and more prone to tearing; the vagina gets drier, more susceptible to infection, and—with loss of elasticity—less able to shrink and expand, less accommodating to the insertion of a penis. (Mickey Rooney on Ava Gardner: "She was unique down there, like a little warm mouth.") In postmenopausal women who aren't receiving estrogen, the vagina becomes smaller in length and diameter. Women's breasts sag and mammary gland tissue is replaced by fat, which aggravates the sagging and is accompanied by wrinkling. The nipples become smaller and get erect less easily. Stretch marks in the breast grow darker. Fat accumulates in the torso, especially near the waist, neck, arms, and thighs—which creates uneven bulges, except in the face, which loses fat and creates a hollower visage. (A friend of Laurie's told her, "At forty, a woman must choose between her face and her ass: nice ass, gaunt face; good face, fat ass.") Women's skin wrinkles, dries, and thins. Men have a thicker dermis than women do, which may be why women's facial skin seems to deteriorate more quickly. Premenopausal women typically show no loss of bone density; postmenopausal women show a faster rate of bone loss than men of comparable age.

For women ages 20 to 40, vaginal lubrication after sexual arousal takes 15 to 30 seconds; for women 50 to 78, it takes 1 to 5 minutes. For younger women, the vagina expands without pain during arousal; for older women, there's a limit to the expansion. Increased blood flow causes the labia minora in younger women to become red; in older women, there's no reddening. For younger women, the clitoris elevates and flattens against the body; in older women, this doesn't happen. For younger women, during orgasm, the vagina contracts and expands in smooth, rhythmic waves, usually 8 to 12 contractions in approximately 1-second intervals, and the uterus contracts. For older women, there are only 4 to 5 contractions, and when the uterus contracts, it's sometimes painful. Older women return to a pre-arousal state much more rapidly.

When men turn 40, the tissues in the back of the prostate gland atrophy and the muscle degenerates, replaced by inelastic connective tissue. A hard mass sometimes appears on the prostate, causing men to produce less semen and at a lower pressure. For many men, the gland cells and the connective tissue in the middle of the prostate overgrow, causing pain during urination. Enlargement of the prostate gland occurs in almost all men, including my father (who had prostate surgery at 85), and the hormone changes that accompany this enlargement can result in various diseases, including cancer. Rates of testicular cancer peak in the 30s, then decline sharply. More inflexible connective tissue grows on the surface of the penis, whose veins and arteries become more rigid. With the reduced blood flow, men find it increasingly difficult to produce and maintain erections. One physician calls the brief, violent upsurge of sexual desire in old men the "final kick of the prostate."

Men ages 20 to 40 need 3 to 5 seconds to achieve an erection when stimulated; for men ages 50 to 89, it takes 10 seconds to several minutes. Younger men quickly feel the need to ejaculate; older men feel less of a need to ejaculate, even over several episodes. For younger men during orgasm, the urethra contracts 3 to 4 times in one-second intervals; semen travels 1 to 2 feet. For older men during orgasm, the urethra contracts 1 to 2 times; ejaculation is 3 to 5 inches, with less semen and a smaller amount of viable sperm. The proportion of immature sperm increases over time. Young men return to a pre-arousal state in anywhere from a few minutes to a couple of hours, in two stages; older men return in a couple of seconds, in a single stage.

On the upside: the oldest verifiable father was 94 at the birth of his last child; the oldest mother was 66.

On the upside, somewhat more viscerally: my father, at 70, telling me a couple of years after my mother's death, "I've been more active this year with Sarah [his new paramour] than I'd been the previous twenty-five with your mother, and I don't mean once a night. I mean two or three times a night most every night of the week and then again in the morning."

Memento Mori

Hair is produced in the skin's hair follicles. A follicle contains more than just hair-producing cells. The melanocytes deposit their pigment in the root of the hair, coloring the hair shaft proteins as they're made. If pure melanin is made, you'll have brown to black hair. If an analogue of melanin called phaeomelanin is made, your hair will be red or blond. If the cells quit functioning altogether, your hair will be white.

There's really no such thing as gray hair. Your hair turns white, not gray. The gray hues you think you see are actually only the intermediate steps as this process advances unevenly across your scalp. The amount of gray you perceive depends on how much of your original hair color mixes with the white.

Everybody has a million hair follicles; only about 100,000 follicles have hair growing from them (blonds slightly more, redheads slightly fewer). The other 900,000 follicles are resting. Each strand of hair grows six inches a year, eventually reaches two to three feet in length, and has its own blood supply. As you age, the density, diameter, and strength of your hair decrease; fewer hairs grow, more rest; you lose hair on your scalp and gain it on your face; and your hair can change not only in color but in texture: your hair can go from straight to curly. Men's eyebrows get thicker, and hair sprouts on the inner canal of the outer ear.

Because they have less estrogen to counteract their bodies' testosterone, postmenopausal women grow facial hair; by age 55, about 40 percent of women grow hair above their upper lip. As women age, they have less armpit hair, which, in older women, often disappears. Armpit hair disappears in most post-menopausal Japanese women. Pubic hair vanishes in a small percentage of women over age 60.

Approximately 100 hairs fall out of your head each day, more during the fall and fewer during the spring. Hair loss is the result of changes in the levels of hormones. If you lose hair, you're more sensitive to these changes in hormone levels. People whose parents experienced hair loss are more likely to lose their hair. One in four women loses some of her hair.

Because of a gradual decrease in adrenal secretion—which begins, for both men and women, in the late 20s—the cells that manufacture hair protein, the germ centers, are selectively destroyed or deactivated. When the affected hair is shed, no replacement occurs.

Forty million American men are bald. Thirty percent of 55-year-old men are bald; 60 percent of 65-year-old men have experienced significant hair loss. Both men and women view bald men as weaker and less attractive than men with a full head of hair. Seventy-five percent of men feel self-conscious about their baldness, and 40 percent wear a hat to hide their baldness. Hair transplants are the most common plastic surgery for men.

There's no cure for baldness. The *Ebers Papyrus*—dating to 4,000 B.C., one of the oldest written documents—advised Egyptian men to treat baldness with a magical potion composed of sea crab bile, blood from the horn of a black cow, burned ass hoof, and the vulva and claws of a female dog.

Woody Allen says, "The best thing to do is behave in a manner befitting one's age. If you are sixteen or under, try not to go bald."

Harlan Boll, a publicist for celebrities, says, "There wasn't as much pressure on men like Bob Hope or Frank Sinatra to look young. Even today this is true. If they keep their hair, they pretty much have it made."

While campaigning for Bush-Cheney, former Wyoming senator Alan Simpson, who's bald, said about Kerry-Edwards, "Everybody is given a certain amount of hormones. If you want to spend yours growing hair, that is your business."

My father has been bald since his early 40s, is unusually self-conscious about the fact, and is fond of saying that the only cure for baldness is a baseball cap, which he wears around the clock, indoors and out. Although I've repeatedly explained to him that a man inherits baldness at least in part from his maternal grandfather, he frequently apologizes for bequeathing to me a bald head. Throughout my 30s I did all the usual boring things: applied Rogaine, studied glossy brochures featuring color photos of weaves, transplants, and men and women in hot tubs. Several years ago, I stumbled upon the shaved-head-and-goatee approach, which I must say I like. It's an acknowledgment of death rather than a denial of death (as, to take an extreme example, the comb-over is). Your head becomes an early memento mori.

The Trouble with Being Food

Your taste buds regenerate; cells within the taste buds die every ten days and are completely replaced. Even if a nerve that forms taste buds is destroyed, other buds will form around the new nerve that replaces it. However, it takes more molecules of a certain substance on your tongue for you to recognize the flavor later in adulthood. As you get older, you enjoy food less. Whenever I visit, one of the first things my father always wants me to do is drive him to a specialty market, where he buys gourmet health food. I'm not sure he enjoys food anymore, but he's obsessed with efficient fuel for his body, that amazing machine. He talks with his mouth full and sprays food so often and so far that Natalie, Laurie, and I take turns sitting across from him at restaurants. Natalie has suggested building a portable sneeze-guard.

Nevertheless:

In Britain in 1991, 13 percent of men and 16 percent of women were obese—twice the number of 10 years before. Half the British population is now overweight; more than 20 percent are obese. In the U.K., snack-food consumption has risen 25 percent in the last 5 years.

More than 60 percent of Americans are overweight or

obese; 127 million people are overweight, 60 million are obese, and 9 million are severely obese. American adults are now, on average, 25 pounds heavier than they were in 1960; the average man has gone from 166 to 191 pounds, while the average woman has gone from 140 to 164 pounds. I doubt my father has ranged more than a few pounds over or below 155 since World War II. More women than men are obese (34 to 27 percent). The average 10-year-old boy weighed 74 pounds in 1963; he now weighs 85 pounds. The average 10-year-old girl weighed 77 pounds in 1963; she now weighs 88 pounds.

In 1980, the government recommendation was 1,600 calories a day for women and 2,200 for men; women now consume 1,877 calories a day and men consume 2,618. In 1970, each person ate 1,497 pounds of food; in 2000, each person ate 1,775 pounds. In the United States, health care costs for treating obese adults amount to $100 billion a year. In 2004, obesity caused 300,000 deaths.

Was my father ever not as skinny as a (third) rail? His meals very nearly always consist of oatmeal and juice for breakfast, a sandwich and a bowl of soup for lunch, "a lean piece" of fish or chicken for dinner. Has he ever taken a second helping of anything? Has he ever not grumbled before reluctantly accepting an offer of dessert? Has a day ever gone by in which he didn't exercise a couple of times? On long family car trips, did he ever not get out every few hours and execute a hundred jumping jacks, to the admiration and/or puzzlement of other travelers on the highway?

I live across the street from a fundamentalist church, and on certain melancholy Sundays I'm filled with empathy for the churchgoers. Adulthood didn't turn out to have quite as much shimmer as we thought it would. For an hour a week, they're hoping to get caught in a little updraft; who can blame them?

Leonard Michaels wrote, "Life isn't good enough for no cigarette"—which is precisely how I've come to view my relationship to sugar. *Today was a disaster*, I tell myself at least twice a week, stopping at a café that makes the most perfect Rice Krispies Treats, *but this tastes delicious.* "Eat dessert first," as the bumper sticker says, "life is uncertain." Quentin Tarantino, asked why he eats Cap'n Crunch, replied, "Because it tastes good and is easy to make." Cap'n Crunch, Rice Krispies Treats: I'm addicted to refined sugar in its less refined forms: breakfast cereal, cookies, root beer floats, licorice, peanut brittle, et al., ad nauseam—kid stuff.

When I'm happy, I consume sweets to celebrate. When I'm upset, I eat treats as consolation. I'm therefore rarely without a reason to be in the throes of sugar shock. I don't drink. I don't smoke. I don't do drugs. I do sugar, in massive doses. So what? Who doesn't? What's the harm? I still stutter slightly, and much of the glory of sugar overload is the way it mimics the biochemical frenzy of a full-blown block and crystallizes it into the pure adrenaline of a brief, happy high (followed quickly by a crash). To me, sugar consumption is a gorgeous allegory about intractable reality and very temporary transcendence.

Everything I Know I've Learned from My Bad Back

Intractable reality (ii): I'm not thrilled to acknowledge that I date the origin of my back problems to the period, 14 years ago, when I repeatedly threw Natalie, then an infant, up in the air and carried her around in a Snugli. It's a dubious etiology, since another cause would surely have come along soon enough; my back, one physical therapist has explained to me, was an accident waiting to happen. It makes perverse sense, though, that in my own mind Natalie and my back are intertwined, because dealing with a bad back has been, for me, an invaluable education in the physical, the mortal, the ineradicable wound.

When he became a father, Jerry Seinfeld said, "I can't get enough of my baby, but let's make no mistake about why these babies are here. They're here to replace us. They're cute, they're cuddly, they're sweet, and they want us out of the way."

I wish I got to indulge in the luxury of being lionized as Atlas by Natalie, but I can't. I'm still quite good at unscrewing tight bottle caps and pinning her arms when I'm tickling or wrestling her. However, if she's sitting atop someone's shoulders on a walk in the woods or getting tossed around in the pool, they're going to be someone else's shoulders, or it's going to be someone else in the pool. At parties, I look first for a chair, since I can't stand for more than a few minutes. I can't hula hoop with Natalie or dance with Laurie. Trying to jog, I usually get pins and needles down my right leg. When we take trips, Laurie has to carry the heavy luggage; at home, she moves the furniture. Atlas I ain't.

You might suspect—I might suspect—Laurie definitely suspects—that maybe I just have a pathetically low pain threshold. And yet my back doctor assures me that with my back, some people play golf and tennis while others have been on disability for 15 years. I fall about in the middle: I've never missed a day of work because of my back, but I certainly complain about it a lot; it's weirdly toward the forefront of my consciousness. I'm not so much a hypochondriac as a misery miser, fascinated by dysfunction. A couple of years ago, I heard an elderly woman, interviewed on the "Apocalypse" episode of *This American Life*, say she welcomed entering the kingdom of heaven because she would finally be granted relief from her incessant physical pain. While I was listening to this, I was driving, my back was killing me every time I turned the steering wheel, and at that moment, I must admit: I could relate.

My father has never even tweaked his back, never had a single physical ailment until the last few years, and yet he's not prone to expressing gratitude for his near-century of good health ("I've had to see more doctors from 94 to 97 than I did from 0 to 94"). Over the last decade I've gone to innumerable physical therapists and doctors. One doctor said I should have back surgery immediately; he had an opening later in the week. Another doctor said all I had to do was perform one particular leg-lift exercise that Swedish nurses did, and I'd be fine. One therapist said I should run more; another therapist said I should run less. One said that human beings weren't built to sit as much as I sit; another said people were never meant to stand upright. One thought I would need to keep seeing him for years and years; another criticized me, after a few months, for not cutting the cord. I used to feel that everything I know I learned through my lifelong struggle with stuttering; I now feel this way about my damn back. Gerald Jonas's book about stuttering is called *The Disorder of Many Theories*. Back Theory seems to suffer from the same Rashomon effect: as with almost every human problem, there is no dearth of answers and no answer.

A few days after 9/11, I saw a back doctor who, unlike 95 percent of doctors I've ever seen, presents himself as a person rather than as an authority figure; ask him how his day is going and he'll say, "Terrible; no one's getting better." He, too, has a bad back, and when he drops his folder, he'll squat down to pick it up, the way back patients are instructed to do, rather than just lean over, the way everyone else does. When I speak to most doctors, I feel slightly or not so slightly crazy, whereas I feel like a person, like myself, when talking to Stan Herring (great name—sounds like a figure from my dad's Brooklyn childhood, like a character from a Malamud story). At my first appointment with him, he emphasized how many of his patients with bad backs carve their entire identity out of the fact that they're patients; they'd have no idea what to do with their lives otherwise. The WTC suicide bombers were, to Dr. Herring, similar to professional patients; their entire existence was given structure and purpose by the fetishization of their pain, their victimhood. The message was subtle, but I got it: don't let yourself become a suicide bomber.

Herring recommended that I see a physical therapist with the unlikely name of Wolfgang Brolley, who goes by the name "Wolf" and looks and moves in a rather lupine way as well. As I am, he's bald (with a shaved head), bespectacled, and goateed, but he's elfin where I'm tall and lanky/clanky. I feel somewhat similar to Herring, who's Jewish and self-deprecating; Wolf is Irish, Chicago-born, passionate, earnest, views himself unself-consciously as a healer, goes to Zen retreats around the globe. I give him an essay I wrote about my adulation of Bill Murray (that death-haunt); he gives me an article he read about the international black-market slave trade. He directs the Center for Physical Arts and Rehabilitation, which features framed quotations from ancient Chinese philosophers and Christian mystics. He's not my buddy; he's something of a taskmaster. When he measured my hamstrings' flexibility—lack thereof— he couldn't help it: he snorted. One morning, when I called to say I felt too bad to come in for my appointment, he said, "You have to come in—that's what I'm here for," and gave me electronic stimulation and a massage. One of my favorite experiences in the physical world is a massage from Wolf.

I used to throw my back out completely—the classic collapse on the sidewalk and yowl to the heavens—but now, thanks in large measure to the Stan-and-Wolf program, I seem to have it under control to the point that my back never goes out completely anymore. (Knock on lumbar.) I sit on a one-inch foam wedge on my chair and get up every hour to do exercises or at least tell myself I do or at least take a hot shower or apply an ice pack or a heat pad. I sleep on my side, on a latex mattress; upon waking, I don't just sit up but rather first "find my center" (there really is such a thing, I'm pleased to report). Wolf keeps reminding me that neither he nor Dr. Herring has a solution: I have to become my own authority and view my recovery as an existential journey. I reassure him that I do, I do. I see going to the drugstore to get toothpaste as an existential journey.

And what existential journey hasn't been aided by chemistry? I've been in and out of speech therapy all my life, but nothing has mitigated my stuttering as effectively as taking 0.5 mg. of alprazolam before giving a public reading. The ibuprofen, the muscle relaxants have certainly helped my back, but the Paxil has been transformative.

At first I strenuously resisted Dr. Herring's prescription, primarily because my father has suffered from manic depression for most of his adult life. In the summer of 1956, my mother was pregnant with me, which caused my father to confess his fear that I was going to be too much of a burden for him because he had a history of depression.

"What do you mean?" my mother, who was a young 31, asked. "You get down in the dumps every now and again?"

"I think I'm on the road to having it licked," he said, "but after the war, then again during a brief period of unemployment before we met, I needed a little electroshock to get me through some bad patches."

Living with a manic depressive wasn't like living with a drug addict. It wasn't like living with a funeral. Last December, Laurie received a card that showed the words "Merry Christmas" being manufactured by a bunch of goofy little guys who looked like Santa's sugar battalion. It was more like that: just knowing every lake is man-made and sooner or later needs to be emptied. For several years my father would be fine and funny and athletically buoyant; then one day he'd come back with an entire roll of negatives of the freeway. Once, in Sacramento on behalf of the poverty program, he mailed me an epistle consisting entirely of blank pages—for no real reason that I could make out. Another time, I was looking for some leftovers in the fridge and came across a note Scotch-taped together, sticky with bloodstains, like advertisements for a sympathetic reader.

My mother packed his suitcase, and he waved shy good-byes like a boy leaving for camp.

However, Herring assured me that I wasn't being "secretly" treated for depression; Paxil has apparently been used to treat chronic pain for more than a decade. For the last several years I've been taking 10 mg. of Paxil a day. I worry a little about becoming a grinning idiot, but I figure I already have the idiocy part down, and I'm so far over on the grouchy side of the continuum that a little grinning isn't going to kill me.

Maybe it's all just the pure dumb rush of selective serotonin reuptake, but now, rather than endlessly rehearsing how my life might have been different, I tell myself how grateful I am for my life—with Laurie and Natalie and our relative health and happiness together. (Knock on lumber.) I'm newly in love with Laurie—aware of her weaknesses and accepting of them, because I'm so blisteringly aware of my own. I go to sleep with a night guard jammed between my teeth, a Breathe Right strip stretched across my nose (to mitigate snoring), and a pillow tucked between my legs. I walk around with an ice pack stuck in one coat pocket and a baggie of ibuprofen in the other. I'm not exactly the king of the jungle.

I like the humility and gravity and nakedness of this need, for—and this is apparently a lesson I can't relearn too many times—we're just animals walking the earth for a brief time, a bare body housed in a mortal cage. For his 50th birthday party, a friend rented a gym around the corner from his house, and I played basketball for most of the night as if I'd somehow been transported back to my 20s—"Backward, turn backward, O Time, in your flight, / Make me a child again just for tonight!" I was, according to Laurie, "running around like a colt," although, of course, a couple of weeks later I aggravated my back and was out of action for a few days. At least I'm now in action. My back will always hurt a bit, or rather the pain will always come and go. "Pain is inevitable," Dr. Herring likes to say. "Suffering is optional." When I quoted the line to Laurie, she said, "Thank you, Dr. Herring." A while ago, I asked Wolf why I have a bad back. He explained that the ability to walk upright was a key evolutionary adaptation for mankind, but vertebrae that are aligned in the same direction as the force of gravity often become compressed, leading to pinched nerves and ruptured disks. Then he said, "In your case, though: bad attitude." He was joking, but I think I got it.

Notes on the Local Swimming Hole

Swimming is by far the best tonic I've found yet for my back. I'm not a good swimmer—I do the breaststroke or elementary backstroke in the slow lane—but when I took a two-week break from swimming, I was surprised how much I missed it. When I returned to the pool, I realized it's where I get, as Evelyn Ames says in *Postcards from the Edge*, "my endolphins." I can hardly bear Sunday, when the pool is closed.

Outside the Green Lake Community Center are the healthy people—the gorgeous rollerbladers and runners and power walkers doing laps around a large lake in the middle of the city, the buff basketball players, the junior high baseball players, the yuppie Ultimate Frisbee players, the latte drinkers checking one another out, the Euro-cool soccer players, the volleyballers, the softball players. The indoor pool is the wetland of the maimed—home to those bearing canes, knee braces, neck braces—for who else would be free or motivated to be here at, say, 1:00 P.M. on Wednesday? I'm joined by people recovering from knee surgery, spinal surgery, car accidents; obese people who weigh themselves daily but never seem to lose a pound; a man in a wheelchair with his faithful dog barking at any potential interference; another wheelchair-bound man whose assistant is an almost cruelly cheerful Nordstrom shoe salesman; the Walrus Splasher (a huge guy with a handle-bar moustache whom we're all trying to build up the courage to approach about the tidal waves he sends our way as he pounds the water); and a pre-op transsexual from New Jersey who, day by day, is wearing more and more feminine attire and is sticking out his butt and chest with greater self-confidence. He's the one who told me the locker room was closed one day owing to an outbreak of leprosy; it turned out to be just a homeless guy who had shat his pants. Nearly everyone here is trying to come back from something; you can feel it in the men's locker room, where we don't talk that much.

The good swimmers while away too much time talking; they're not desperate, as the rest of us are, to claw their way back into shape by doing their assigned 36 laps (one mile). The good swimmers have an uncanny ability to skid across the top of the water, while the rest of us plunge down, down, down. The falling apart of our bodies; the perfection of youthful bodies; the pool is, for me, about one thing: the tug of time.

Every swimmer seems lost in his or her own water space (accidentally touching someone's toe or shoulder always feels thrillingly, wrongly intimate). I'm never so aware of the human perplexity as when I'm at Green Lake with my fellow bodies. We're all just trying to stay alive; we have no greater purpose than glimpsing a shadow of ourselves on the surface as we glide underwater. What is the point of floating? To keep floating. I feel the weightless, gorgeous quality of existence.

Until very recently, my father would swim at least 15 laps every day, diving headfirst rather than sashaying his way in, as I do. Now, though, he can hardly manage a stroke or two across the width of his condo's pool without his arthritis forcing him to stop and clutch his leg. He's always been addicted to terrible puns; now, he keeps playing with variations on the word "arthritis." *Arthur, write us. Author, write us. Author, right us.* There's no author, we both know, and there's no way he can right us. Earlier this year, it was just the two of us alone in the pool. I was doing laps and flip turns—my back was feeling weirdly trouble-free for the moment—while he was tottering in the shallow end. After just a few minutes, he got out, toweled off, and headed over to the sauna, carrying the sports page.

Sex and Death (iii)

As soon as animals, including humans, reach sexual maturity, many of their functions weaken. These weaknesses appear in humans beginning at age 25.

With the salmon and octopus and many other plants and animals, reproduction is, in effect, willful suicide. After reproduction, the body is a useless shell, so it's discarded. The body is, for all intents and purposes, the host, and the reproductive system is the parasite that brings the body to its death.

As the biologist E. O. Wilson says, "In a Darwinian sense, the organism does not live for itself. Its primary function is not even to reproduce other organisms; it reproduces genes, and it serves as their temporary carrier. Samuel Butler's famous aphorism, that the chicken is only an egg's way of making another egg, has been modernized: the organism is only DNA's way of making more DNA."

Bats live longer than rats, but they reproduce more slowly. Birds live longer than ground-dwelling mammals, but flightless birds have short lives. Some turtles and tortoises live longer than humans. Organisms exposed to high risk invest little in maintenance and a lot in reproduction, whereas organisms exposed to low risk do the opposite.

Virgin male and female fruit flies live longer than fruit flies that reproduce. According to Luc Bussière, a zoologist at the University of Zurich, the best predictor of male crickets' mating success is the quantity of time spent calling females. "We heightened this behavior by manipulating dietary intake," he says. "For males on high-protein diets, it had the effect of promoting their promiscuity and reducing their longevity. They literally knocked themselves out trying to impress female crickets. For humans, this might seem counterproductive because we don't want to die young. We want to live long lives. But for animals the goal isn't living longer; it's to reproduce." The survival instinct and the reproductive instinct are opposed.

Women who live longer have, on average, lower levels of fertility. Childless men and women, though, don't live longer than those who are mothers and fathers. You can't choose not to have children and thereby gain extra years of life by redirecting your resources for reproduction into efforts at self-maintenance. Your genes make you disposable but have not left you the flexibility to choose to live a longer life by not propagating them. My father has frequently complained to me—without the least self-consciousness or irony—about what a toll it took on him to have to earn a living. "Let's put it this way," he once said. "I wanted a good life available on terms that did not offend. It hasn't always worked out that way. There were jobs I wasn't exactly crazy about, worked at them because there were bills to pay, a lot of financial obligations and responsibilities."

In an experiment on white mice gender-segregated by an electric fence, the males backed off at the first severe shock whereas the females continued to charge the fence until each in turn was electrocuted.

A woman's shapely hips are a sign of childbearing potential; fat deposits serve as an energy source during pregnancy. A few weeks after Natalie was born, I was walking home from the market, carrying diapers, baby food, etc. Noticing a young, attractive, glammed-up woman wearing a halter top and driving a red convertible, I viewed her in terms I would never have considered before: something approaching awed appreciation that she was doing all she could to perpetuate the species.

So many Hollywood movies are barely disguised procreation myths—getting the most fertile couple to come together. To take one among thousands of examples, in Otto Preminger's film *Laura*, gossip columnist Waldo Lydecker lives in language and can't engage life. Shelby Carpenter, a gigolo, is too dumb to have any grasp on life, expressing himself only through clichés. Homicide detective Mark McPherson knows what life's about and so is able to maneuver through it successfully, despite its dangers and the inevitable conclusion (death). Lydecker winds up killing the wrong woman, then getting shot. Carpenter childishly submits to an older woman's maternal embrace. McPherson and Laura, at movie's end, are ready to breed.

Which is all our obsession with human beauty is, anyway: an evolutionary adaptation for evaluating others as potential producers of our child. Male college students, shown photos of more and less attractive women, are far more likely to volunteer for altruistic and risky acts for a beautiful woman. Attractive women are 10 times more likely than plain women to "marry up." Not news. But mothers with attractive babies spend more time holding their baby close, staring into their baby's eyes, than mothers with babies judged less attractive; the latter spend more time tending to their baby's needs and are distracted much more easily. Babies born prematurely—who often have falsely mature faces—are imagined to be difficult and irritable, and people are less willing to volunteer to take care of them. So, too, a study of abused children under court protection in California and Massachusetts found that a disproportionate number of them were "unattractive." When people are asked to approach a stranger and stop when they no longer feel comfortable, they stop nearly two feet away from attractive people, as opposed to less than a foot from less attractive people: beauty is privileged territory. In youth, my father was extremely handsome, a Jewish prince, and he's never gotten over that fact. When my first novel was published and I had a little book party to celebrate, he didn't attend because he wasn't looking his best. This was in 1984; he was 74.

People will say about an especially pretty little girl, "She's going to be a heartbreaker"—which is, to me, an odd and revealing phrase. What does it mean, exactly? It means that when she grows up, she will use her beauty as a weapon, and she is expected to do so.

In *Survival of the Prettiest*, Nancy Etcoff describes American coots: gray birds whose chicks have orange plumes and bald heads that turn bright red during feeding. The chicks beg for food by flashing their red and orange signs for their mother. When researchers trimmed the orange plumes, the drabber chicks got less attention and food from the mother, who fed the more colorful chicks first. When human mothers give birth to high-risk, low-weight twins, they invariably favor the healthier twin, soothing, holding, playing, and vocalizing more with the twin more likely to survive. A mother has limited resources; she needs to know how much to invest in her new baby without endangering herself and the lives of her other children.

A mortal animal is a germ cell's way of making more germ

cells, thereby optimizing the likelihood that they'll fuse with germ cells of the opposite sex. The continuation of the germ line is the driving force of natural selection; longevity of individual animals is of secondary importance. Animals are selected through evolution for having physiological reserves greater than the minimum necessary to reach sexual maturation and rear progeny to independence, but once this goal has been accomplished, they have sufficient excess reserve capacity to coast for a period of time, the remainder of which is called your life span. You're a salmon without portfolio.

In 1930, one in five cancer patients survived; in 1940, one in four; in 1960, one in three; in 1990, 40 percent survived. Now, 50 percent survive. One out of every eight American women will develop breast cancer in her lifetime, and the risk increases with age. Three of the risk factors are early menstruation, childbirth after 30 or no childbirth, and menopause after 50; you're urged, in other words, to get on stage when expected, hit your lines at the right time, and then exit on cue. Any deviation, and evolution exacts its toll. There's really only one immutable biological law, it has only two imperatives, and it gets stated in dozens of ways: spawn and die.

I was patiently waiting my turn at the pharmacy when a 20-something, accompanied by his pretty, punky girlfriend, tried to cut in line. I told him to go to the back. He said, "What is this, junior high?" I said, "No, this is the line for the pharmacy, but the way you're acting—" He asked why I couldn't grow hair on my head. I wondered why he hadn't grown any taller. It was a very high-level exchange. He pushed me; I pushed him. He raised his fists and said, "Let's go." Forty years receded, and it was as if I'd returned to 6th grade, the last time I was in a fight: I got a huge adrenaline surge, I could hear my heart thumping, and I couldn't quite catch my breath. I declined the drugstore fisticuffs, but I replied—with the emphatic approval of my middle-aged comrades in line—"Life has rules." It does? I was appalled; it never occurred to me that I would ever say anything remotely resembling this. If life has rules, what are they? At a party recently, I overheard a woman, attempting to seduce a young man half her age, say, "I'm forty-five, but I'm tight." That's pretty much it: sex and death. Reproduction and oblivion.

In *Rabbit, Run*, published when John Updike was 28, he wrote, "The fullness ends when we give Nature her ransom, when we make children for her. Then she is through with us and we become, first inside, then outside, junk. Flower stalks."

Steve Nash, 34, who has been the Most Valuable Player of the National Basketball Association two of the last three years and who is the father of 3-year-old twin girls, says, "I guess I'm learning more how insignificant my life is. I still enjoy my work. I still enjoy my friends and family and relationships, but you realize the girls are so innocent and dependent. You realize your life, in some ways, is over."

Thackeray said, "When one is twenty, yes, but at forty-seven Venus may rise from the sea, and I for one should hardly put on my spectacles to have a look."

A few years ago, I told Laurie that it seemed to me as if so many people our age—48 or a bit older—had started taking "nice pills"; everyone seemed so much more mellow. She said, "It's not them. It's you: you're nicer. And so people seem to you—"

"No," I protested. "No I'm not. I'm a walking blade."

In a short story, Barry Hannah writes about his protagonist, who's in his late 40s, "He still did not know precisely what accounted for it, but some big quiet thing had fallen down and locked into place, like a whisper of some weight. Ned Maxy had been granted contact with paradise, and he could hardly believe the lack of noise."

Joke courtesy of Dr. Herring: There are three kinds of married sex. When you're first married, you're so lusty you have sex in every room in the house. After several years, the passion dies down a little, and you confine sex to the bedroom. After many years, you pass each other in the hallway and say, "Fuck you." One in five married couples has sex less than once a month; I recently heard a woman on the radio suggest that couples should have sex no more often than they do their taxes (quarterly? annually?).

The weak links of the human body are exposed when people survive beyond the reproductive period. For instance, the thymus gland degenerates after your sexual maturation. At age 50, you retain only 5 to 10 percent of the original mass of the thymus, which produces hormones whose levels decline at age 25 and are undetectable after 60.

The weight and size of the uterus decrease after menopause until age 65, when it's half the weight it was at 30. After age 60, men have fewer and fewer erections during sleep. Sexual daydreams decline in frequency and intensity until age 65, when they largely disappear.

Sophocles, in old age, said finally being free of sexual desire was "like escaping from bondage to a raving maniac."

In opposition, again, to all this decline and fall, this piece my father wrote, in his late 80s, for his class:

It's funny how easily you can misjudge people or, more specifically, women. How easy it is to be deceived about

what happens or what's said at a first meeting. After our
first date, I felt that we would become lovers in a month.
In a worst-case scenario, six weeks or two months. I met
Virginia for the first time at a Palo Alto senior center
where I'd gone to a lecture on the future of the novel.
I got there late and the only seat was in the back row,
which turned out to be next to her. When the lecture and
question-and-answer and coffee-and-cookies periods
were over, I said I'd escort her to her car in the parking
lot, since it was late. When we got to her car, I mumbled
the ritualistic "Glad to have met you" and was prepared
to leave, when she reached into her purse and pulled out
a card with her name and phone number on it. She asked
me to call her.

Two weeks later I did. It was on a Friday night and I
asked her about seeing her the next night and quickly
apologized about calling on such short notice. She said
there was no need to apologize, invited me to her place
for dinner, and said I'd be as welcome as the flowers in
May. Damn if she didn't repeat that silly "flowers in May"
line every single time I called to arrange the time and
place of our next meeting.

On that first evening together, I helped her wash the
dishes after dinner. She said something about me being a
real handy man to have around the house and added that
her husband, a busy Santa Clara doctor, never washed or
dried a dish in all the years they were married. This
remark of hers about my being so helpful was the perfect
opening for one of my sure-fire laugh-getters and I
promptly said, "I'm not one of those men who thinks a
woman's place is in the stove. No macho male me." She

chuckled appreciatively and said something about my being a nice guy and added she was glad she ran into me at the senior center that night.

At 10:00, Virginia suggested we watch the news. We sat on the sofa and I held her hand. After about 15 minutes, I tried to kiss her—nothing serious, but she pulled back and pleaded with me to go slowly and be patient and told me I was the first man she'd dated since her husband's death three years ago. She followed that up with the words I was to hear over and over: "Milt, I need a little more time."

No problem, I assured her that first night. We watched the rest of the news holding hands. Not bad, I remembered saying to myself during the 45-minute drive home. Give it time and it will work out. Couldn't miss. I was a lonely widower with a lot of time and a little money and she was a lonely widow, anxious for companionship. Plus. So she hinted, not very subtly.

Several months later, after attending a lavish 40th anniversary banquet for a couple Virginia and her late husband had known for many years, we got back to her apartment about midnight. I had had more than my usual quota of drinks that night and had danced with her five or six times; that was way above my quota, too. She seemed to cling to me during those slow numbers; she had never done that before.

I felt a little more romantic, a little hornier when we got back to the apartment. As soon as we got inside the apartment and closed the door, I grabbed for her clumsily, but she parried my thrust, saying she had to powder her nose and wanted to get out of her confining and dressy evening clothes. I read into her words a suggestion that the patience I had displayed, when she had asked early on in our relationship for more time on my part, would pay off.

In preparation, I took off my dark jacket and draped it over the chair. The same with my black bow tie. I also took my shoes off and pushed them under the sofa, then waited like an eager schoolboy.

Virginia came out of the bathroom, put a tape with some nice dreamy music on the stereo, and sat down beside me. I grabbed her, pushed her back on the sofa, and reached for her mouth. She pushed me away, asking me to please take it easy. Then I tried to slide my hand inside her bathrobe and fondle her ample breasts.

And that's when she said what she said on our very first date: "Please don't rush me, Milt. I need time." But that night I wasn't buying what I was convinced was a line or patent ploy. I erupted like Vesuvius, shouting, "Exactly how much more time do you need? Your husband's been dead for three years now, right?" And what was all this phony business about the wonderful marriage she and her husband had for the nearly 40 years they were together? I reminded her that she'd told me one night that she'd had three extramarital affairs, one of them lasting about seven years; the marriage was slightly less than idyllic. "Lady, it's high time to get on with the rest of your life, whether it's with me or anybody else."

That's when she asked if we couldn't be friends, and could we just forget about the sex?

That did it. I snatched my coat and tie off the back of the chair, reached under the sofa for my shoes, and stormed toward the door, where I delivered my parting shot. I told her I'd had enough of her games and play-acting. Six months of frustration, six months of an antiseptic, sexless relationship was a bit much. I told her that I needed and wanted the love and warmth of a good and fulfilled relationship and I thought that she wanted the same thing. "If I wanted a friend," I said, "I would have bought a dog." I don't know where I first heard or read that line, but, make no mistake, I thought to myself, it was a barn burner. It left her with her tongue literally hanging out, poised to say something in rebuttal, but she remained speechless. We never, needless to say, saw each other again.

Hoop Dream (viii)

I once felt animal joy in being alive and I felt this mainly when I was playing basketball and I only occasionally feel that animal joy anymore and that's life. I'm 51 and I feel this way; I don't think my father started feeling this way until he was 95.

Old Age and Death

Decline and Fall (iii)

Samuel Johnson wrote to a younger friend, "When I was as you are now, towering in the confidence of twenty-one, little did I suspect that I should be at forty-nine what I am now."

At age 50, your ability to perceive vibrations in the lower part of your body is significantly decreased. The nerves that conduct information signals to the brain are also diminished. Every decade after age 50, your brain loses 2 percent of its weight. You have difficulty learning things and you remember less and less. Memory per se—the actual encoding of information—isn't diminished in a healthy, older person, but retrieval can be an excruciatingly slow process and take many more attempts. Older people are more susceptible to distraction, have trouble coordinating multiple tasks, and have decreased attention spans. In simple tasks and common situations, the old do fine, but when exercise or other stress is added, they often struggle. Perhaps this is why some older people, finding it harder to cope, tend to start searching for comfort rather than excitement.

Evelyn Waugh said, "Old people are more interesting than young. One of the particular points of interest is to observe

how after fifty they revert to the habits, mannerisms, and opin-
ions of their parents, however wild they were in youth."

"At fifty, everyone has the face he deserves," said George
Orwell.

Virgil, author of *The Aeneid*, died at 50.

As you age, your eye lens clouds over (cataract). The cells of
the optic nerve can be damaged by glaucoma or macular
degeneration. Forty-two percent of people ages 52 to 64, 73
percent of people 65 to 74, and 92 percent of people over 75
need reading glasses. My father, after having cataract surgery
20 years ago, didn't really need glasses anymore.

Shakespeare died at 52.

John Wayne said, "I'm fifty-three years old and six foot
four. I've had three wives, five children, and three grandchildren. I love good whiskey. I still don't understand women,
and I don't think there is any man who does."

You gain weight until age 55, at which point you begin to
shed weight (specifically, lean tissue, muscle mass, water, and
bone). More fat now accumulates in your thighs and less in your
abdomen. Your extremities become thinner and your trunk
thicker. Middle-aged spread isn't only the result of increased
fatty tissue; it's also caused by losing muscle tone and your skin
literally thinning out as each skin cell loses its robustness.

Dante died at 56.

Between 50 and 60, your visual memory declines slightly;
after 70, it declines substantially.

Noel Coward, advising a middle-aged friend to stop dieting, said, "This is a foolish vanity. Youth is no longer essential
or even becoming. Rapidly approaching fifty-seven, I find
health and happiness more important than lissomeness. To be
fat is bad and slovenly, unless it is beyond your control, but
however slim you get you will still be the age you are and no

one will be fooled, so banish this nonsense once and for all. Conserve your vitality by eating enough and enjoying it."

"The years between fifty and fifty-seven are the hardest," said T. S. Eliot. "You are being asked to do things, and yet you are not decrepit enough to turn them down."

In late middle age, the skin in your hands becomes less sensitive to touch. Your skin cells regenerate less often. The skin weakens and dries, the number of sebaceous glands declines dramatically, and all of the tissues of the skin undergo some change: you get wrinkles and gray hair. Wrinkles don't come from age, though. They come from sunlight, which slowly maims the face, causing wrinkles, mottling, and loose skin. Although the skin loses elasticity and heals wounds more slowly with advancing age, it never completely wears out.

At 59, Neil Young said, "When you're in your twenties, you and your world are the biggest thing, and everything revolves around what you're doing. Now I realize I'm a leaf floating along on top of some river." My father hates this way of thinking, finds it defeatist.

Your blood cholesterol increases. The ability of the blood to maintain a normal level of glucose declines with age. At 60, you've lost 25 percent of the volume of saliva you normally secrete for food; it becomes more difficult to digest heavy meats.

When you're 60, you're 20 percent less strong than you were in middle age; at 70, you're 40 percent less strong. You lose more strength in the muscles of your legs than in your hands and arms. You also tend to lose your fast-twitch abilities—a sprinter's contractions—much more rapidly than your slow-twitch abilities—a walker's contractions. (Some of this decline can be stalled by exercise, but by no means all. As a rule, the variability between individuals increases with age: almost all younger people will have, for instance, the same kidney function and be able to solve a problem at approximately the same speed, but with older people, some will be normal, others will be very impaired, and most will be somewhere in between.)

Emerson said, "'Tis strange that it is not in vogue to commit hara-kiri, as the Japanese do, at sixty. Nature is so insulting in her hints and notices, does not pull you by the sleeve, but pulls out your teeth, tears off your hair in patches, steals your eyesight, twists your face into an ugly mask, in short, puts all contumelies upon you, without in the least abating your zeal to make a good appearance, and all this at the same time that she is moulding the new figures around you into wonderful beauty which of course is only making your plight worse."

The year Zola died, he said, at 62, "I am spending delightful afternoons in my garden, watching everything living around me. As I grow older, I feel everything departing, and I love everything with more passion."

The PR flak Harlan Boll defends his lying about his celebrity clients' ages by saying, "The American public doesn't really forgive people for getting older." Which is of course true. Jackie Kennedy said if she knew she was going to get cancer at 65, she wouldn't have done all those sit-ups. In jail, O. J. Simpson bemoaned to his girlfriend that the once admirable, apple-like shape of his posterior had collapsed into middle-aged decrepitude. Gravity sucks.

By the time you reach 65, you've lost 30 to 40 percent of your aerobic power. The walls of your heart thicken, and you're more likely to develop coronary disease. Sixty percent of 60-year-old men, and the same percentage of 80-year-old women, have a major narrowing in at least one coronary artery.

A stiffening in the walls of the major arteries results in a progressive increase in blood pressure, which imposes an increasing load on the heart. Since the heart has to work harder for each heartbeat and use more energy, the overall efficiency of the cardiovascular system drops significantly. One and a half million Americans suffer a myocardial infarction each year. Seventy percent of heart attacks occur at home. If you survive a heart attack, you're virtually guaranteed to die eventually of a heart-related illness. My father had a heart attack at 86 (more on this later), had his heart stop beating for 30 seconds during electroconvulsive therapy at 92, and several months ago he was hugely, irrationally afraid that his upcoming colonoscopy (he'd had some bloody stools, and his doctor wanted to figure out what was triggering his ceaseless seesawing between diarrhea and constipation) would cause his heart to stop for good.

At 65, you've lost one ounce of your three-pound brain and one-tenth of your brain cells. The motor area of the frontal cortex loses 50 percent of its neurons, as does the area in the back controlling vision and the area on the sides controlling physical sensation. The gyri—the twisting, raised convolutions in the cortex within which you do much of your thinking—experience the greatest atrophy. The brain of a 90-year-old is the same size as that of a 3-year-old. The details of the new Medicare drug benefits program perplex and annoy everyone, including me, but they've completely defeated my dad; he no longer grasps concepts he used to grasp. His mental operations do seem, on many channels, newly simple.

Joints age owing to deterioration in cartilage, tendons, and fluid. The fluid contained within joints begins to thin. More friction is created. Nearly everyone age 65 or older shows some abnormality of the joints; one out of two people has moderate to severe abnormality. One-third of American women over 65 have collapsed vertebrae as a result of bone thinning, or osteoporosis. The more bone you have as an adult, the less likely you are to develop osteoporosis. (Generally speaking, it's best and easiest to head off aging's ravages when you're young, which is exactly when you aren't thinking about them.)

When you're a young adult, the reflex that tells you it's time to urinate occurs when your bladder is half full. For people over age 65, the message isn't received until your bladder is nearly full.

Five percent of the U.S. population live in a nursing home. When I asked my father a dozen years ago whether he'd ever want to consider moving into a retirement home in Seattle, he replied, "I don't know how long I'll be working. Right now, I can get out there and cover the games (basketball, baseball, football, etc.) and turn in two or three pieces each week. I'm not down to my last two bits. Still have some money in my savings account, plus the money I get from Social Security and the annuity I bought in 1977, plus what I get each month from the paper. I'm like the man betting in Las Vegas who says, 'I hope I can break even. I sure could use the money.' I miss you and Laurie and Natalie and Paula and Wayne [my sister and brother-in-law, who live forty miles south of Seattle in Tacoma] more than words can say. But life at Woodlake offers me many activities. And there's also the god-awful Seattle weather. I look on the retirement home as a terminal stop. We old-timers joke about those places, calling them 'God's waiting room.' Where the average age is deceased. (Gallows humor.) So I would like to spend the rest of my days in my own apartment here in Woodlake. For one, I couldn't afford a retirement home. I'm not ready for that type of living. Or spending. Here I quote again from my steno notebook of memorable phrases (don't know who wrote it or where I read it): 'Each man picks his own hill to die on.' My 'hill' certainly would not be a retirement home. Ideally, it would be out on a golf course. Bing Crosby and a couple of other well-known people have died on golf courses. Nice way to go if you've lived a good share of years. Not fifty or even sixty."

There are now more people in the United States over 65 than ever before. Only 30 percent of people ages 75 to 84 report disabilities—the lowest percentage ever reported.

Five to 8 percent of people over 65 have dementia; half of those in their 80s have it. One of many dementias and the most common, Alzheimer's affects 1 in 10 Americans over 65, 1 in 2 people over 85. Alzheimer's patients are more likely to have had a low-stress (i.e., mentally unstimulating) job. Zero sign, though, as yet of Alzheimer's in my father: he's still reading and rereading Robert Caro on Robert Moses, Philip Roth on Newark, Arnold Rampersad on Jackie Robinson, Gar Alperovitz on the decision to drop the atom bomb.

According to Noel Coward, "The pleasures that once were heaven / Look silly at sixty-seven."

At 68, Edmund Wilson said, "The knowledge that death is not so far away, that my mind and emotions and vitality will soon disappear like a puff of smoke, has the effect of making earthly affairs seem unimportant and human beings more and more ignoble. It is harder to take human life seriously, including one's own efforts and achievements and passions."

"Tomorrow I shall be sixty-nine," William Dean Howells wrote to Mark Twain, "but I do not seem to care. I did not start the affair, and I have not been consulted about it at any step. I was born to be afraid of dying, but not of getting old. Age has many advantages, and if old men were not so ridiculous, I should not mind being one. But they are ridiculous, and they are ugly. The young do not see this so clearly as we do, but some day they will."

Thomas Pynchon says, "When we speak of 'seriousness' in fiction, ultimately we are talking about an attitude toward death—how characters may act in its presence, for example, or how they handle it when it isn't so immediate. Everybody knows this, but the subject is hardly ever brought up with younger writers, possibly because given to anyone at the apprentice age, such advice is widely felt to be effort wasted."

Fifteen years ago, on a gorgeous spring day, my father and I jogged down my block. A school bus of middle-school girls rounded the corner. He puffed out his chest, let out his kick, put himself on display. Rather than ooh or aah or whistle or applaud or ignore him, several girls stuck their heads out the windows in the back of the bus and did the cruelest thing possible: they laughed.

"You're only young," AC/DC sing on *Back in Black*, "but you're gonna die."

In your late 60s, you eat less. Your metabolic rate decreases slightly. Men lose 3 percent of their skeletal weight per decade (my father now weighs 150); women lose 8 percent. Throughout adult life, men lose about 15 percent of their total mineral density; women, 30 percent. The diameter of your forearm shrinks, as does the diameter of your calves.

The density of your skin's circulatory systems—veins, capillaries, arterioles—is reduced, which is why old people feel cold sooner. Also, your skin functions less well as a barrier because the skin is thinner—like wearing too light a coat. As you age, your facial skin temperature falls. For older people, a comfortable temperature is 10 to 15 degrees higher than it is for a younger person.

. . .

Each day of your adult life, you lose 30,000 to 50,000 nerves and 100,000 nerve cells. Over time, your heart, lungs, and prostate enlarge. The level of potassium in your body declines. After age 70, your ability to absorb calcium is dramatically reduced.

Tolstoy wrote to his wife, Sonia, who was 16 years younger than he was, "The main thing is that just as the Hindus, when they are getting on toward sixty, retire to the forests, and every religious man wants to dedicate the last years of his life to God and not to jokes, puns, gossip, and tennis [jokes, puns, gossip, and tennis: paging Milton Shildcrout . . .], so I, who am entering my seventieth year, long with all my heart and soul for this tranquility and solitude." He died at 82 when he collapsed in a train station, in flight from Sonia, with whom he'd been quarreling.

At age 70, the mass of your corneal lens is three times larger than it was when you were 20, which causes you to be more farsighted; after age 70, you become more nearsighted. The lens becomes thicker and heavier with age, reducing your ability to focus on close-up objects. Your sensitivity to contrast declines, as does your ability to adapt to changes in light. As you get older, the corneal hue takes on a yellow tint, reducing your ability to discriminate among green, blue, and violet. Blues will get darker for you and yellows will get less bright. You'll see less violet. As painters age, they use less dark blue and violet.

Sir Francis Chichester, after sailing around the world at age 66, said, "If your try fails, what does that matter? All life is a failure in the end. The thing to do is to get sport out of trying."

Men and women over age 75 suffer ten times the incidence of strokes as do those between 55 and 59.

The professionally world-weary Gore Vidal said, apropos of having to sell his house on a hill in Ravello, Italy, because he was no longer able to climb the steps, "Everything has its time in life, and in a year, I'll be 80. I'm not sentimental about anything. Life flows by, and you flow with it or you don't. Move on and move out."

When you're very young, your ability to smell is so intense as to be nearly overwhelming, but by the time you're in your 80s, not only has your ability to smell declined significantly but you yourself no longer even have a distinctive odor. You can stop using deodorants. You're vanishing.

"I think the old need touching," says the social historian Ronald Blythe. "They have reached a stage of life when they need kissing, hugging. And nobody touches them except the doctor." At 82, E. M. Forster said, "I am rather prone to senile lechery just now—want to touch the right person in the right place, in order to shake off bodily loneliness." The last few years, whenever I hug my father hello or good-bye, he cries and cries, shuddering.

Voltaire wrote to a friend, "I beg you not to say that I am only eighty-two; it is a cruel calumny. Even if it be true, according to an accursed baptismal record, that I was born in November 1694, you must always agree with me that I am in my eighty-third year." When you're very old, you want to be thought even older than you actually are: it's an accomplishment. At 67, my father purchased an annuity that he would have broken even on if he'd died at 76; having outlived the actuarial projections by 21 years so far, he tells everyone he meets how much he's made on it. He buttonholes strangers and informs them that he's only 3 years from the century mark.

At 83, Sibelius said, "For the first time I have lately become aware of the fact that the period of our earthly existence is limited. During the whole of my life this idea has never actually come into my mind. It occurred to me very distinctly when I was looking at an old tree there in the garden. When we came it was very small, and I looked at it from above. Now it waves high above my head and seems to say, 'You will soon depart, but I shall stay here for hundreds more years.'"

At 85, Bernard Baruch said, "To me, old age is always fifteen years older than I am."

At age 90, you've lost half of your kidneys' blood-filtering capacity.

You grow increasingly less likely to develop cancer; the tissues of an old person don't serve the needs of aggressive, energy-hungry tumors.

By 90, one in three women and one in six men suffer a hip fracture, which often triggers a downward spiral leading to death. Half will be unable to walk again without assistance. My father, on the other hand, walked a mile to and from the library—carrying books in each direction—until he was 95.

At that age, his moles were disappearing—a mole typically lasts 50 years—and in their place, a couple of "cherry moles," which look like cherries and the technical name for which is "hemangiomas," appeared on his chest. His doctor said he thought my dad's hemangiomas (benign tumors composed of large blood vessels) were beautiful. Easy for him to say; he's a whippersnapper of 67. My father found the cherry moles as distressing as if he were a teenage girl with an array of pimples on her chin.

At 97, a month before dying, Bertrand Russell said to his wife, "I do so hate to leave this world."

Bernard de Fontanelle, a French scholar, who died at 100, said, "I feel nothing except a certain difficulty in continuing to exist."

Aristotle described childhood as hot and moist, youth as hot and dry, and adulthood as cold and dry. He believed aging and death were caused by the body being transformed from one that was hot and moist to one that was cold and dry—a change which he viewed as not only inevitable but desirable.

In *As You Like It*, Jaques says, "And so from hour to hour, we ripe and ripe, / And then from hour to hour, we rot and rot." The Sullivan County (NY) Yellow Pages informs its readers that "the process of living means that we are all temporarily able-bodied persons." The 34-year-old American poet Matthea Harvey writes, "Pity the bathtub its forced embrace of the human form." Time, to paraphrase Grace Paley, makes a monkey of us all—even my father, fight it fiercely though he does.

The Thing About Life Is That One Day You'll Be Dead

John Donne said, in a sermon, "We are all conceived in close prison, and then all our life is but a going out to the place of execution, of death. Nor was there any man seen to sleep in the cart between Newgate and Tyburn—between the prison and the place of execution, does any man sleep? But we sleep all the way; from the womb to the grave we are never thoroughly awake."

Charles Lamb said, "The young man till thirty never feels practically that he is mortal."

John Ruskin said, "Am I not in a curiously unnatural state of mind in this way—that at forty-three, instead of being able to settle to my middle-aged life like a middle-aged creature, I have more instincts of youth about me than when I was young, and am miserable because I cannot climb, run, or wrestle, sing, or flirt—as I was when a youngster because I couldn't sit writing metaphysics all day long. Wrong at both ends of life . . ."

The eponymous hero of Chekhov's *Uncle Vanya* says, "I'm forty-seven now. Up to a year ago I tried deliberately to pull the wool over my eyes so that I shouldn't see the realities of life, and I thought I was doing the right thing. But now—if you only knew! I lie awake, night after night, in sheer vexation and anger that I let time slip by so stupidly during the years when I could have had all the things from which my age now cuts me off."

Edward Young wrote, "At thirty man suspects himself a fool; / Knows it at forty, and reforms his plan / At fifty chides his infamous delay, / Pushes his prudent purpose to resolve; / In all the magnanimity of Thought / Resolves, and re-resolves; then dies the same."

Picasso said, "One starts to get young at the age of sixty, and then it's too late."

At 62, Jonathan Swift said, "I never wake without finding life more insignificant than it was the day before."

Leonardo da Vinci, who died at 67, said, "Here I thought that I was learning how to live, while I have in reality been learning how to die."

Barry Hannah says, "The calamity is that we get only seventy-five years to know everything and that we knew more by our guts when we were young than we do with all these books and years and children behind us."

At 78, Lord Reith, the first general director of the BBC, said, "I've never really learned how to live, and I've discovered too late that life is for living."

The seventeenth-century moralist Jean de la Bruyère said, "There are but three events in a man's life: birth, life, and death. He is not conscious of being born, he dies in pain, and he forgets to live."

Regrets only:

My father came up from the Bay Area to visit for the week-end and my Father's Day present, six days late, was box seats to a Mariners game. I was new to Seattle and this was the first time I'd been inside the Kingdome which, with its navy blues and fern greens, looked to me like an aquarium for tropical fish. The Kingdome reminded my father of "dinner theater," and he wanted to know where John Barrymore was. My dad was turning 79 the following month; he wanted—at 80—to quit his part-time job and drive a Winnebago cross-country, then fly to Wimbledon to eat strawberries and cream.

The sixth-place Mariners were playing the last-place Tigers on Barbecue Apron Night. Watching batting practice, we folded and unfolded our plastic Mariners barbecue aprons, which smelled disconcertingly like formaldehyde, and we ran through all the baseball anecdotes he'd told me all my life, only this time—because I pressed him—he told each story without embellishment. He'd always said that he played semi-pro baseball and I had images of him sliding across glass-strewn sandlots to earn food money; it was only guys from another neighborhood occasionally paying him 10 bucks to play on their pickup team and throw his "dinky curve." He used to say that he was team captain for an Army all-star baseball team that toured overseas, and as a kid I convinced myself that he spent 1943 in Okinawa, hitting fungoes to Ted Williams and Joe DiMaggio. He was only traveling secretary, the most prominent player on the team was a Detroit Tiger named Pat Mullins, and it was fast-pitch softball Stateside.

My father used to look almost exactly like Dodgers coach Leo Durocher ("Nice guys finish last."). When we were living in Los Angeles, the garbageman supposedly shook my father's hand and said, "Sorry to hear about your marriage, Mr. Durocher." Durocher had been recently divorced from the actress Laraine Day; the garbageman was being sympathetic in the male manner—so went the story. And for some reason I always thought my father stood atop the trash in the back of the truck, hefted garbage cans with one hand, and cursed The Fishbowl Which Is Hollywood, whereas in actuality he immediately told my mother about impersonating Leo Durocher, she cautioned him against stringing along the innocent garbage collector, and he chased down the truck to explain and make amends.

Before the game, there was a "Peace Run" around the field—some sort of marathon-for-a-cause which I didn't quite catch because the PA system sounded like it was being filtered through a car wash—then the umpires strolled onto the Astroturf. This is Seattle, so they weren't booed even a little, though, which disappointed my father. In 1940, he was the star student at a Florida umpire school run by Bill McGowan, who said my father could become "another Dolly Stark" (i.e., a Jewish umpire), but before reporting to Class D ball my father begged off, citing his poor night vision. He wound up umping Brooklyn College–Seton Hall games and once got whacked over the head with a walking stick when he called someone's favorite son out at home with two on, two out, the score tied, and the light, I guess, failing. My father's favorite Bill McGowan story concerned the time McGowan, a former amateur boxer, grew weary of Babe Ruth's grousing and, during the intermission of a doubleheader, challenged the Babe to a fight. The Babe backed down. The hero of my father's stories is usually someone else. It's rarely him.

The Mariners scored three in the first. Keith Moreland looked painfully uncomfortable at third for the Tigers. Ken Griffey Jr. made a nice catch in the fifth. The game was devoid of much interest, though, for either of us (longtime Dodger fans)—as my father said, "like watching a movie when you don't care what happens to the characters."

Assigned to write an essay on his favorite sports team, he wrote, "I swore undying loyalty to the Brooklyn Dodgers when I was 8 or 9, maybe even younger. Looking back over the bridge of many years, it seems to me I took up my allegiance for the Dodgers with my mother's milk. My feelings for the team ranked one emotional peg below what I felt for my family." Just as the walls of my childhood bedroom were covered with pictures of the Los Angeles Dodgers, his were covered with pictures of the Brooklyn Dodgers. Zack Wheat. Dazzy Vance. Wilbert Robinson. His essay continued:

Ebbets Field, where they played, was the temple, and baseball—which they played at times with heartbreaking inefficiency—was a secular religion for me.

I learned the Dodgers' lineup before I mastered the ABCs. And I became skilled at keeping an intricate scorecard before I could handle numbers in the classroom. Just a matter of priorities.

To give you an idea of the kind of fan—make that nut—I was: During the season, I would rush to the door of our apartment at 6 in the morning to grab the *New York World* to find out how the Dodgers had made out the day before. If they won, I'd be all smiles, sing a little song quietly so as not to wake the rest of the family, but if they lost, I'd sit at the kitchen table and sob. My sobs would be heard by my father, who would get up and try to comfort me.

"Milt," he'd say, putting his arm around me, "who are these Dodger people you're carrying on about? Why do you take it so hard? What happened—did somebody die?"

"You don't understand, Pop," I'd say through my tears. "They're *my* team."

"Whaddya mean, *your* team? They're not related to us, right? No, they're a bunch of strangers. You've only seen them once when your brother Abe took you to a game. Like I said, nobody died, the rent is paid, and everybody is in good health, thank God."

Usually by this time my mother would get up to begin preparations for breakfast for the family. "Leave him alone, Sam," she'd say. "He'll get over it. Today it's the Dodgers," which my mom pronounced to sound like "Deitches"—which, freely translated, is "Dutch," or "German," in Yiddish. "Tomorrow it'll be something else."

I didn't get over it, as my mom predicted, until I was 21 and other things claimed my loyalty and passion: girls, the trade union movement, journalism.

But before I gained some perspective and finally realized "it was only a game," I suffered; oh how I suffered: my beloved Brooklyn Bums, as they were affectionately called, lost more of them than they won. In the middle of a Dodger losing streak, I'd ask myself why God, in His infinite wisdom, didn't make me a Yankee fan.

He moved to Los Angeles in 1946, and while my mother was suffering blackout spells during a late summer heat wave in 1955, he flew back to New York, ostensibly to attend his father's 85th birthday party but, more particularly, to attend the World Series and, even more particularly, watch the Dodgers finally beat the Yankees and, more particularly still, watch Jackie Robinson steal home under Yogi Berra's tag. I have my father's pictures of press row at Yankee Stadium. Look at the snap-brim hats.

In our family mythology, this flight of my father's was always painted in the darkest of colors, and yet when I was a child I, too, would look first thing each morning at the box scores, then cry ickily into my cereal if the Dodgers had lost. I remember defacing my Ron Perranoski baseball card when he failed to hold a huge lead going into the ninth, pushing over my grand-father's television set when it broadcast Dodger right fielder Ron Fairly's misplay of an easy flyball into a home run over the low right-field wall at Dodger Stadium, engaging in a weird sort of mock-Ophelia thing at the beach after the fiasco of the 1966 Series against the Orioles. What was this obsession we had with the Dodgers? "For me, it comes out this way," my father wrote me the week after this Father's Day visit. "I wanted the Dodgers to compensate for some of the unrealized goals in my career. If I wasn't winning my battle to succeed in newspapering, union organizing, or whatever I turned to in my wholly unplanned, anarchic life, then my surrogates—the nine boys in blue—could win against the Giants, Pirates, et al. Farfetched? Maybe so. But I think it has some validity. In my case. Not in yours."

Oh, no; not in mine; never in mine.

Although the Kingdome (since demolished) had, even by ballpark standards, notoriously bad food, we decided to stand in line at the concession anyway, not because we were so hungry but because we needed something to do while a wave was going around the stadium. My father and I both got a hot dog and a beer, and we shared a bag of peanuts—which came to an amazing amount of money, for a meal my father said had the nutritional quotient of a resin bag. To my father's astonishment, I topped off this indigestible dinner with a chocolate malt, which looked almost purple and tasted as bitter as coffee. We returned to our seats. The wave was still rising and falling, or maybe it was a new wave.

Sixty years before, he was a sports stringer for the *New York Journal-American;* now he was covering the Little League, Pony League, Colt League, men's fast-pitch softball, and women's softball for a suburban weekly. Three days before he came up to visit, he was trying to take a photograph of a Little Leaguer stealing third base and the catcher's throw hit my father in the ankle, breaking three blood vessels. He was proud of his bruised ankle and he kept showing it to me, repeatedly reenacting the scene, saying with a sportswriter's mix of hyperbole and mixed metaphor, "It blew up like an egg."

He always used to send me the column he wrote for his tennis club newsletter. This was by far my favorite lead: "A hundred members and guests attended the annual Tennis Club meeting and, to coin a forgettable phrase, a helluva time was had by all and sundry. (Especially Sundry, who seemed to be having the time of his life.)" When I'm in certain moods, this Borscht Belt humor can completely convulse me.

Just as in order to express some sort of vague rebellion we didn't stand up during the National Anthem, during the seventh-inning stretch we didn't stretch, either, although I couldn't help but watch the "full-matrix scoreboard," which was flashing images of fans stretching. All 15,000 fans in the Kingdome were watching the scoreboard, waiting to find out whether they were beautiful enough to be broadcast, since virtually without exception the images were Pacific Northwest–perfect: sleepy babies wearing Mariners caps, energetic grandparents, couples kissing. The moment people were shown, they pointed at the screen, then they pointed at themselves pointing at themselves on the screen, then everyone pointed at them pointing at themselves pointing at themselves on the screen. I continued looking at the scoreboard, wanting my chance to point at myself pointing at myself on the screen, and then I looked over at my father, who hadn't been watching the screen at all. He was tidying up his scorecard. He was no longer looking to be lifted onto an empyrean matrix; he just wanted to eat strawberries and cream at Wimbledon the summer of his 80th birthday. (He never went.)

"Presley, Martinez, and Vizquel coming up for the Mariners," he said, and we went to the bottom of the seventh.

Boys vs. Girls (iv)

Between the ages of 55 and 64, men are twice as likely as women to die in car accidents and four times as likely to commit suicide. Losing a job, separating from my mother, battling manic depression, my father would sometimes threaten that he was going to drive to the Golden Gate Bridge and jump off, but the threat never seemed real: he's a survival machine.

Between ages 35 and 54, the ratio of men to women is even, then it increasingly favors women. In 1990, less than half of people in their 30s were female, but 80 percent of centenarians were women. Now, 90 percent of centenarians are women. Will my dad become a centenarian? He dearly wants to (see above; see below).

Men have much higher testosterone levels than women, which makes them more susceptible to cardiovascular disease—the main reason they don't live as long. Testosterone also suppresses the immune system and makes it more difficult for males to resist infection. Premenopausal women have 20 percent less blood in their bodies than men and a correspondingly lower iron load. Iron ions are a source for the formation of "free radicals," molecules formed during food metabolism that can harm the body; a lower iron load leads to a lower rate of aging, cardiovascular disease, and other age-related diseases in which free radicals play a role. Testosterone is the cause of the spike in the sex-mortality ratio at puberty (the trigger for boys' destructive and self-destructive acts) and then increases blood levels of LDL ("bad" cholesterol) and decreases levels of HDL ("good" cholesterol), putting men at greater risk for heart disease and stroke. Estrogen has exactly the opposite effect, in addition to acting as an antioxidant, which neutralizes radicals.

Throughout the animal kingdom, species show the same sex difference in life span: females nearly always live longer than males, with some exceptions (for instance, hamsters, guinea pigs, and wolves). Female longevity is more essential, from an evolutionary perspective, than the prolonged survival of males. In a mammal, the male's contribution to child raising is often much less than the female's (my father's role wasn't to be a caretaker but to be cared for); without her, the child will probably die. Female sperm whales' life span is 30 years longer than male sperm whales'. For orcas, there's a 20-year difference. If a male calf survives to its first birthday, it can expect an average life span of 30 years, while a female can expect an average life span of 50. The maximum estimated life span for female orcas in the wild is 70 to 80; for males, 50 to 60.

A species' life span is correlated with the length of time its young remain dependent on adults. The necessity for female longevity in the human reproductive cycle has determined the length of the human span. The longer a woman lives and the more slowly she ages, the more offspring she can produce and rear to adulthood. For men, on the other hand, reproductive capacity is mostly limited by their restricted access to women. Men are stronger, taller, faster, and less likely to be overweight than women—older men have 20 percent higher maximum oxygen capacity than older women do—but women, as a group, live longer than men. In the United States, newborn girls have a life expectancy of 7.7 more years than newborn boys. At 65, it's 4.4 years' difference in life expectancy; at 75, 2.9; at 85, 1.4. The more vulnerable males are eliminated from the aging population faster than females are. Who else but my dad would have survived the third rail?

In Latin America and the Caribbean, life expectancy for women is 72; for men, 65. In Europe, life expectancy for women is 76; for men, 67. In the Middle East, the figures are 71 and 67; in Africa, 52 and 50; in Asia, 66 and 63. Male life expectancy continues to exceed female life expectancy only in such countries as Bangladesh, India, and Pakistan, where female infanticide and bride-burning are common practices.

Women have more chronic nonfatal conditions (arthritis, osteoporosis, and autoimmune disorders), but men have more fatal conditions such as heart disease and cancer. At all ages, women detect odors better than men (when a friend asked many of her women friends what they remembered most when they thought of their mothers, nearly all of them associated Mom with a smell); the ability to identify odors declines earlier and more rapidly in men than in women. Epilepsy attacks males and females in approximately equal numbers, but the death rate from it is 30 percent higher in males. Females suffering from the same infectious diseases as males die at a much lower rate. Among women and men who smoke equally large numbers of cigarettes, women are more resistant than males to lung cancer and heart disease. Men's higher metabolic rate, compared to that of women, reduces their longevity (according to his doctor, my father has the heart of a 70-year-old man). Women have a higher ratio of brain weight to body weight than men do; women's higher brain weight to body weight increases their longevity. British geneticist Steve Jones believes that the male of the species—given his shorter life span, declining sperm counts, and the decrepit nature of the Y chromosome—may be doomed to oblivion in 10 million years. Jones's theory isn't widely held, but still, as Jack Nicholson has said, "They're smarter than us, they're stronger than us, and they don't play fair."

Women have lived longer than men since at least the 1500s. Between 1751 and 1790, in Sweden, the average life expectancy at birth was 36 for women and 33 for men. However, only in the last 100 years has it become clear that women's life expectancy exceeds that of men; until then, so many women died in childbirth that their life expectancy, as a group, was nearly the same as that of men. In West Africa, more women still die in pregnancy than from all violent causes. In the developing world, the lifetime risk of dying from pregnancy is 1 in 32; in the developed world, the risk is 1 in 7,000. Every year, more than half a million women die during pregnancy or childbirth; 10 million suffer injuries, infection, or disability. Since 1900, life expectancy for women worldwide has increased 71 percent (compared to 66 percent for men), but mortality from lung cancer has tripled in women in the past two decades. Because more women now smoke, drink, and work outside the home, there's been a striking deceleration in the extension of female life expectancy. In America, life expectancy for women is now 80 years, for men it's 75 years, and the gap is steadily closing. As women behave more like men, they live less long.

Chronicle of Death Foretold

When you're dying, your blood often becomes extremely acidic, causing muscles to spasm. The protoplasm is too compromised to sustain life any longer. You may emit a short series of heaving gasps; sometimes your larynx muscles tighten, causing you to bark. Your chest and shoulders may heave once or twice in a brief convulsion. Your eyeballs flatten out because their round plumpness depends on the blood that's no longer there. When you die, you don't—contrary to legend—lose 21 grams in weight; if human beings have a soul, it doesn't weigh anything.

In extreme cases such as severe trauma, exactly when someone is pronounced dead depends on where he or she dies. In the United States, some states say that brain activity is the only criterion; in other states, it's respiratory and cardiac activity. In France, the brain has to be silent for 48 hours. In the former Soviet Union, patients needed to flatline for five minutes. According to Dr. Henry Beecher, "Whatever level of electrical brain activity we choose, it's an arbitrary decision." Doctors have more personal anxieties about dying than people in any other profession.

. . .

For people in the 50-to-59 age group, the death rate is 56 percent less than it is for the general population; 50-to-59-year-olds are just too busy to die.

In a study of 1,000 Major League Baseball players who played between 1876 and 1973, the players had a death rate 25 percent lower than that of men overall. A 1986 study of 17,000 Harvard graduates, ages 34 to 74, found that death rates declined as energy expenditures increased, up to 3,500 calories a week; above that, and death rates increased slightly. (Swimming vigorously for an hour burns approximately 500 calories.)

Cardiovascular disease kills 40 to 50 percent of people in developed countries. Cancer kills 30 to 40 percent; car accidents kill 2 percent; other kinds of accidents kill another 2 percent. When my father and mother separated and he was mixing antidepressants with alcohol, he drove smack into a garbage truck (accidentally? intentionally? never really explained), totaling his car but leaving him without a scratch— the Energizer Bunny. In the United States, heart disease kills 1 in 40 65-to-69-year-olds, 1 in 27 70-to-74-year-olds, 1 in 11 80-to-84-year-olds, and 1 in 7 people 85 years old and over. In 1949, 50 percent of American deaths occurred in the hospital; in 1958, 61 percent; in 1977, 70 percent; now, 80 percent. Septic shock (extremely low blood pressure due to extensive infection in a vital organ) is the leading cause of death in intensive care units in the U.S.: 100,000 to 200,000 deaths a year. Only 36 percent of Americans have living wills. In the U.S., elderly white men commit suicide at a rate five times the national average. One in five doctors receives a request for physician-assisted suicide, and 10 percent of those respond by agreeing to assist.

In the Paleolithic age, half of all babies died before reaching their first birthday; mothers often died giving birth. For most of the last 130,000 years, life expectancy for human beings was 20 years or less. The huge majority of people ever born died early in life from an infectious or parasitic disease. In the second century A.D., the average life span was 25; at least one-third of babies died before reaching their first birthday. Two hundred years ago, the average life span for an American woman was 35; a hundred years ago, it was 48; it's now 80—the largest, most rapid rise ever.

In 1900, 75 percent of people in the United States died before they reached age 65; now, 70 percent of people die after age 65. From 1900 to 1960, life expectancy for a 65-year-old American increased by 2.4 years; from 1960 to 1990, it increased 3 years. In England in 1815, life expectancy at birth was 39 years. In Europe during the Middle Ages, life expectancy at birth was 33 years, which is approximately the life expectancy now for people in the least developed countries.

Very old age in antiquity would still be very old age now. In the sixth century B.C., Pythagoras lived to be 91. Heraclitus of Ephesus died at 96. The Athenian orator Isocrates died at 98. The average life span has increased since the industrial revolution, but primarily because of declining rates of childhood mortality. In Sweden during the 1860s, the oldest age at death was usually around 106. In the 1990s, it was around 108.

In developed countries, 1 in 10,000 people lives beyond the age of 100. In the U.S., there were 37,000 centenarians in 1990; there are now around 70,000. The majority of American centenarians are female, white, widowed, and institutionalized, were born in the U.S. of Western European ancestry, and have less than a ninth-grade education. Ninety percent of current American centenarians have an annual income of less than $5,000 (excluding food stamps, federal payments to nursing homes, and support from family and friends); they often say they were never able to afford to indulge in bad habits. In many ways, this is true of my father: he grew up relatively poor, our family was always barely making ends meet, and he now lives a spartan life on a fixed income.

On his 100th birthday—five days after which he died—Eubie Blake said, "These docs, they always ask you how you live so long. I tell 'em, 'If I'd known I was gonna live this long, I'd have taken better care of myself.'"

"Who wants to be a hundred?" asked Henry Miller, who died at 89. (That's my dad waving wildly in the third row.) "What's the point of it? A short life and a merry one is far better than a long one sustained by fear, caution, and perpetual medical surveillance."

Woody Allen, on the other hand, has said, "I don't want to achieve immortality through my work. I want to achieve immortality through not dying. I don't want to live on in the hearts of my countrymen. I would rather live on in my apartment."

Another joke courtesy of Dr. Herring:

A priest, a minister, and a rabbi are discussing what they'd like people to say after they die and their bodies are on display in open caskets.

The priest says, "I'd like someone to say, 'He was righteous, honest, and generous.'"

The minister says, "I'd like someone to say, 'He was kind and fair, and he was good to his parishioners.'"

The rabbi says, "I'd want someone to say, 'Look, he's moving.'"

Eighty-eight percent of Americans say that religion is important to them; 82 percent of Americans believe that prayer can heal. Ninety-six percent of Americans say they believe in God or some form of universal consciousness; 72 percent believe in angels; 65 percent believe in the devil. In one study of 3,000 American men and women over age 65, people who attended church were half as likely to have strokes as those who never or almost never attended services. In another study, of nearly a thousand American men and women admitted to a coronary care unit, those who received remote, intercessory prayer fared better than those who did not. Those on the receiving end of prayers were less likely to require antibiotics. In a survey of 92,000 American men and women, people who attended church more than once a week were far less likely to get certain diseases than those who attended infrequently. Over a five-year period, the death rate from heart disease was twice as high among those who didn't go to church very often as it was for those who frequently attended. During a three-year period, infrequent attendees were twice as likely to die of emphysema and four times as likely to die of cirrhosis of the liver as were frequent attendees. In a study of 230 older American men and women who had just had cardiac surgery, people who said they received strength and comfort from practicing their faith were three times more likely to survive than those who didn't.

When my father was a boy, he studied the Four Kashas—the Four Questions—in Hebrew School and so had no problem reading the Hebrew text and translating it when his father called on him, during Passover Seder, to recite the Four Questions: Why is this night different from all other nights of the year? On all other nights we eat leavened bread or unleavened bread; why on this night do we eat only unleavened bread? On all other nights, we eat bitter herbs and other bitter food; why on this night do we eat only bitter herbs? On all other nights we eat either reclining or straight up in our chairs; why on this night do we eat only reclining? My father, the youngest of four brothers, was the most adept at Hebrew and, as he says, "basked in the sun of my father's approbation. I, the kosher ham, squeezed every ounce of personal satisfaction out of it." He had a Bar Mitzvah at the Pennsylvania Avenue Synagogue, where he delivered a brief sermon, expressing gratitude on reaching religious adulthood, but his mother had recently died, at age 49, leaving his father and six children, so the ceremony was more somber than festive. (At her funeral, her casket was pulled through the street on a horse-drawn cart, and my father remembers being deeply embarrassed by his father's open display of grief—weeping and pounding the casket.)

My father's father introduced him to Socialism a couple of years later; my father lost God and has been, as he would say, a "devout atheist" the rest of his life. Of late, though, he prefers to call himself an agnostic—"It's all very mysterious, Dave." He also can't say, "When I die . . ." Instead, he says, "If and when the time might come . . ." After that, it's all mumbled, euphemistic evasion.

Cormac McCarthy: "Death is the major issue in the world. For you, for me, for all of us. It just is. To not be able to talk about it is very odd."

Charles de Gaulle said, "The cemeteries of the world are full of indispensable men"—one of my father's very favorite quotations, and mine as well. It's consolation, of a sort: everybody tries, no one wins, everybody dies.

Propertius said, "Among the dead are thousands of beautiful women."

Juvenal: "Weigh the dust of Alexander the Great and the village drunkard, and they'll weigh the same."

Schopenhauer: "We are all lambs led to slaughter."

At 51, Tchaikovsky said, "I am aging fast, I am tired of life, I thirst for quietness and a rest from all these vanities, emotions, disappointments, etc. etc. It is natural for an old man to think of a prospective dirty hole called a grave."

Freud said, "What lives, wants to die again. Originating in dust, it wants to be dust again. Not only the life-drive is in them, but the death-drive as well."

In 44 B.C., Cicero said, "No one is so old that he does not think he could live another year"; he died in 43 B.C. On his deathbed, William Saroyan said, "Everybody has got to die, but I always believed an exception would be made in my case." Edward Young wrote, "All men think all men mortal but themselves." The ancient Indian epic *Mahābhārata* asks, "Of all the world's wonders, which is the most wonderful? That no man, though he sees others dying all around him, believes that he himself will die."

My father's column for the condo tennis club newsletter about his heart attack, at 86:

> I was doing what I had done on Memorial Day since
> memory runneth not to the contrary: playing tennis. It
> was a picture-postcard perfect day. The temperature was
> a comfortable 75, with a light breeze. I felt like a tiger.
> Just another lousy day in paradise.
>
>   My partner, George Tripodes, and I were playing a

match against old friends and rivals Jim Black and Harry Langdon. We won the first set—barely squeaked through at 10–8 and were leading in the second set, 4–3. It was my turn to serve. I quickly jumped into a 40–love lead. I walked from the deuce court to the add court, where I hoped to make it 5–3, when I suddenly felt like an elephant had placed a huge foot on my chest (a standard description, I know, but that's exactly how it felt to me). I paused for a few seconds, saying to myself, "Now what was *that*?" It was like nothing I had experienced in my 86 years on planet Earth. It was, as I was about to learn about an hour later, a heart attack—a relatively mild one, true, but still a full-fledged heart attack.

I wasn't going to let a little old heart attack prevent me from winning my serve or finishing the set. George walked over to me as I was getting ready to serve and asked if I felt okay. "You look a little pale, Milt," he said.

"No problem," I assured him, adding that I wanted him to cover the right hand alley because I was planning—heart attack notwithstanding—to serve the ball into the extreme right corner of my opponent's court.

And that's exactly what I did, drawing a feeble response in return, and sending us into a 5–3 lead, one game away from winning the set and match. Our opponents made it 5–4 and now it was George's serve. We had a tough time winning the sixth and final game; we finally managed it after a couple of long rallies. I wasn't much help to my partner in that final game but never let on for a moment that I was feeling "a little strange."

When the set ended, I didn't bother to shake hands with Jim and Harry. I grabbed my tennis bag and windbreaker and walked back to my building, about 100 yards from the courts. I walked back slowly but somehow managed to make it to my apartment, throwing some cold water on my face, then knocking on the door of my neighbor, Mary Steiner, a retired registered nurse. Mary took my pulse, checked my heartbeat, and immediately called 911.

"You've had a heart attack, Milt," she said very professionally, leaving no room for doubt.

Twenty minutes later I was in an ambulance en route to Peninsula Hospital, where doctors quickly confirmed Mary's diagnosis. I was immediately anesthetized and given an angioplasty—the "balloon" treatment—opening up one of my arteries, which had clogged.

I awoke about two hours later, feeling—believe it or not—absolutely wonderful: a huge load had been lifted from the side of my chest.

The cardiologist, Dr. George Cohen, came by later that afternoon to explain what I had been through and what he had done—the angioplasty—to relieve the pressure. Dr. Cohen asked me, "Is it true that you continued to play another ten minutes after that first big bump? How in hell did you ever manage to do that?"

"I don't know, Doc," I said. "I just had to finish the set and match. Those two guys we were playing had beaten us too many times before and I had to try to balance the books when I had the chance."

"You're something else," said Dr. Cohen.

Two days later I was sent home and three weeks later I was back on the courts, just a little worse for my Memorial Day ordeal.

Tennis, anyone?

Death Is the Mother of Beauty

Neither my father nor I could sleep. We finally figured out how to work the remote for his new TV—a present from my sister and me on his 95th birthday. At 2:00 A.M.:

On channel 2, a movie detective revisited the murder scene.

On channel 4, Retin-A entrapped tretinoin in Microsponge systems.

On channel 7, college girls on vacation in Cancun removed their T-shirts.

On channel 8, the Civil War was reenacted.

On channel 10, Bobby Abreu won the Home Run Derby.

On channel 11, Double D Dolls mud-wrestled.

On channel 12, a university lecturer explained gravity.

On channel 13, the Faith, Health & Prosperity bracelet glittered in the light.

On channel 17, a woman did leg raises.

On channel 20, taffy and ice cream production facilities were profiled.

On channel 22, fat-free desserts tasted as good as regular desserts.

On channel 24, 79 people died in a plane crash; an infant was the lone survivor.

On channel 29, Hercules tossed an enormous boulder.

On channel 30, Miss Teen USA was crowned.

On channel 33, you developed smart abs in just two minutes a day.

On channel 36, Dr. Ellen's Light His Fire and Light Her Fire programs helped your marriage by increasing your energy.

On channel 38, a woman whose teenage daughter died in a car crash found solace in God's love.

On channel 41, a murder victim's body was autopsied.

On channel 42, the CrossBow system offered compound resistance.

On channel 47, Aquafresh toothpaste removed stains.

On channel 49, the Cancer Treatment Centers of America helped you harness your power to fight cancer and win.

On channel 55, two buxom blonde women explained to a thin, balding man why size matters.

On channel 59, the Slim in 6 fitness program helped you lose 20 pounds in 6 weeks.

On channel 63, the Ultimate Chopper was the ultimate time saver.

On channel 64, the Esteem by Naomi Judd System reduced wrinkles, lines, and blotchiness.

On channel 72, the Arthur Ashe Award was given to a terminally ill coach who advised the audience to never give up.

On channel 77, a woman was penetrated from behind by one man while she performed fellatio on another man.

On channel 80, the Youth Cocktail gave you sharper, clearer memory and more flexible joints.

On channel 84, two behemoths competed to pull an enormous ball-and-chain across the finish line.

On channel 85, a suicide bomber killed himself, two civilians, and two U.S. soldiers in Ramadi.

On channel 87, Hair Color for Men got the gray out.

On channel 89, with long life you will satisfy Him and show Him your salvation.

On channel 90, you could have the makeover of a lifetime.

On channel 95, Hollywood celebrities paid $24,000 for Mari Winsor's body-sculpting program.

On channel 99, a horror movie ended with a white curtain blowing in the breeze against a black night.

On channels 2 through 99, we sought but couldn't find a cure for the fact that one day we would die.

Life Is That Which Gives
Meaning to Life

André Gide wrote in his journal, "Every day and all day long, I ask myself this question—or rather this question asks itself of me: shall I find it hard to die? I do not think that death is particularly hard for those who most love life. On the contrary."

Elizabeth Barrett Browning said, "Knowledge by suffering entereth, / And life is perfected by death."

In the journal my mother kept the last year of her life, she wrote, "Of one thing I'm sure: I don't want to live if I can't function, make decisions for myself, and take care of myself. I hope that if I reach that point I'll have the courage to take my life. I feel very strongly that life is a very precious gift and that one should always choose life, but to me life is being able to function. Maybe I'll be able to express this better and more clearly as time goes on." My father frequently alludes to this journal entry and shakes his head in wonder and bafflement and, in a way, pity.

In *Lament for the Makers*, William Dunbar wrote, "Timor mortis conturbat me": the fear of death distresses me.

As a 9-year-old, I would awake, shivering, and spend the entire night sitting cross-legged on the landing of the stairs to my basement bedroom, unable to fathom that one day I'd cease to be. I remember being mesmerized by a neighbor's tattoo of a death's head, underneath which were the words, "As I am, you shall someday be."

Simone de Beauvoir wrote, "From the time I knew I was mortal, I found the idea of death terrifying. Even when the world was at peace and my happiness seemed secure, my 15-year-old self would often turn at the thought of that utter non-being—*my* utter non-being—that would descend on its appointed day, for ever and ever. This annihilation filled me with such horror that I could not conceive the possibility of facing it coolly. What people called 'courage' I could only regard as blind foolishness."

Rousseau said, "He who pretends to look on death without fear lies."

The narrator of Donald Barthelme's story "The School," an elementary-school teacher, says:

One day, we had a discussion in class. They asked me, where did they go? The trees, the salamander, the tropical fish, Edgar, the poppas and mommas, Matthew and Tony, where did they go? And I said, I don't know, I don't know. And they said, who knows? and I said, nobody knows. And they said, is death that which gives meaning to life? And I said, no, life is that which gives meaning to life. Then they said, but isn't death, considered as a fundamental datum, the means by which the taken-for-granted mundanity of the everyday may be transcended in the direction of—

I said, yes, maybe.

They said, we don't like it.

My father has asked me to research the affordability and plausibility of "cryonic suspension." He's willing to die, but he doesn't want to be dead forever.

Hoop dream (ix):

My grandfather, my father's father, Samuel, was a business agent for the International Ladies Garment Workers Union of the CIO, in Westchester. He'd awake at 5:30, have a cup of tea and piece of toast, glance at the newspaper, and leave for the subway at 6:00. He handled workers' grievances and contract negotiations with manufacturers. He'd eat his dinner hurriedly, then be off to his second job—investigator for the neighborhood Eastern Star Credit Union, which he had helped found. At first, the credit union made small loans of $50 and $100 to its members, almost all of whom were recently arrived Russian and Polish immigrants (as was my grandfather, who fled to England in the 1880s rather than face induction into the notoriously anti-Semitic Russian army, which often exiled Jews to Siberia). Several years later, after it was credentialed by the New York State Banking Commission, it was lending $10,000. My grandfather's signature would guarantee the loan if the original borrower failed to make the payment; he'd walk for miles to some homes, and my father would sometimes accompany him. Samuel would return at midnight, sleep five hours, and be up the next morning to take the long subway ride to the factory. He also purchased shirts at wholesale and sold them to his friends for a small profit. As a teenager, my father would help my grandfather lug the boxes of shirts through the streets of their neighborhood. When he was older and had a car, my father would drive him around Brooklyn to collect signatures on loans. My father says, "I never knew where he found the energy to keep up the pace he did." My father says this.

Sam spent Sunday mornings reading the three Yiddish newspapers: *Forward, Der Tog (The Day)*, and *Freiheit (Freedom)*. A Socialist, he introduced my father to notions of "dialectical materialism," "left-wing infantilism," "alienation of the proletariat," and "means of production." He would say, "Milteleh, don't ever forget this: under Communism, man exploits man, while under capitalism, the reverse is true. No matter what fancy words presidents or commissars or kings use, it's money—economics, the cash nexus—that rules the world. Money is the world." For emphasis he would repeat this last formulation in Yiddish: *"Geld ist der veldt."*

My grandfather gave my father *Ten Days That Shook the World*, John Reed's account of the 1917 Russian Revolution, which my father read over and over. In high school history classes, my father would sometimes challenge what the teacher said or the textbooks omitted. When questioned where he got a particular fact or point of view, he would say, as instructed, "My father, who knows whereof he speaks."

"You can tell, Dave, can't you, how his life touched me?" my father likes to say about his father. "There was the sense of doing things for his fellow men; there was the kindly, mediating approach. *Ess vett soch oy spressen*, he liked to say. It will press itself out. It will take care of itself. He couldn't cope with problems. He let them drift, grow, fester, or fly away. Recognize some of your dad's penchants and peccadilloes in that?"

The night before my grandfather's funeral, my father and I wandered around his apartment. I was 7 and had never met him. My grandfather's skinny belts and wide ties hung from hooks in a closet. Badly warped classical record albums were stacked against a wall. His wallet and a Nikon sat atop the stripped bed. His favorite coffee mug was carefully wrapped in plastic, as was, of all things, a brand-new basketball: undelivered present for me, my father figured, and then he fell to pieces.

How to Live Forever (i)

In 1600 B.C., the Egyptian papyrus *Book for Transformation of an Old Man into a Youth of Twenty* recommended a potion involving herbs and animal parts. In ancient Greece, old men were advised to lie down with beautiful virgins. When my father visited me at college, he virtually ignored my girlfriend and focused on her roommate, whom he kept calling "a very attractive young woman." Castration—believed to extend the life span a few years—was popular in the Middle Ages. Eunuchs do live longer than uncastrated men. A sterilized dog or cat, male or female, will live, on average, two years longer than unsterilized dogs and cats. In the early sixteenth century, Ponce de León, age 55, searched for the Fountain of Youth because he was unable to satisfy his much younger wife. Later in the sixteenth century, Francis Bacon thought that if the body's repair processes—that is, our capacity for tissue regeneration and healing and our ability to recover from disease—were perfected, aging could be overcome.

In the nineteenth century, the French physiologist Charles-Édouard Brown-Séquard removed and crushed the testicles of domesticated animals, extracted vital substances from them, then used this concoction to inoculate older people, who reported improved alertness and vitality. When Brown-Séquard, at age 72, injected himself with the extract, he claimed to have better control over his bladder and bowels. He died four years later. Eugen Steinach, a professor of physiology in Vienna in the 1920s, convinced older men that they would be rejuvenated by a vasectomy or by having the testicles of younger men grafted onto their own. Rejuvenation clinics sprang up around the world: surgeons devised a number of anti-aging therapies, including the application of electricity to the testicles and doses of X-rays and radium to the sex organs.

According to Michael Jazwinski, a molecular biologist at Louisiana State University: "Possibly in 30 years we will have in hand the major genes that determine longevity, and will be in a position to double, triple, even quadruple our current maximum life span of 120 years. It's conceivable that some people alive now will still be alive in 400 years."

William Regelson, professor of medicine at Virginia Commonwealth University, says, "As we learn to control the genes involved in aging, the possibilities of lengthening life appear practically unlimited."

Michael Rose, an evolutionary biologist at University of California-Irvine, permitted only those fruit flies that produced eggs later in their life span to contribute eggs to the next generation. (This is equivalent to selecting women age 25 and older to be mothers and then only permitting the daughters who were fertile after age 26 to reproduce, and so on, for many generations.) Each generation of fruit flies lived a little longer than the previous one. The fruit flies from this ongoing program of selective breeding continue to live progressively longer than their ancestors. Rose believes that if a similar experiment could be performed on humans, a measurable increase in life expectancy would be observed within 10 generations.

Fruit flies given resveratrol, an antioxidant found in red wine, live significantly longer than other flies. Molecules in resveratrol called sirtuins mimic the life-extending effects of caloric restriction, which slows aging in mammals. Living creatures are hardwired to reproduce; a low-calorie diet sends a message throughout the body that conditions aren't optimal for reproduction. Cellular defense systems arise and aging slows, preserving the body for better, more reproduction-friendly times. Caloric restriction triggers a release of stored fat, which tells the body it's time to hunker down for survival.

Two thousand people belong to the Calorie Restriction Society, and 10 percent of them have cut their consumption by at least 30 percent. The greatest life extension, as much as 50 percent, comes from starting a severely restricted diet in young adulthood and continuing it throughout life. Starting in midlife and cutting calories 10 to 20 percent yields a smaller benefit. Fasting every other day (while otherwise eating normally in between) also increases average life span. My father, with his lifelong and much trumpeted and unrelievedly austere diet, should have been the founding member of the Calorie Restriction Society. Interviewed by his own paper on his 95th birthday, he focused almost entirely on the importance of nutritional discipline, with special attention to bran muffins.

A near-starvation diet dramatically reduces the incidence of most age-related disease: tumor and kidney problems, brain-deficit problems such as Alzheimer's, and degenerative problems such as Parkinson's. Rats on a 40 percent reduced-calorie diet have a 30 percent longer life span. Monkeys on a reduced-calorie diet—30 percent less for 15 years—live longer and avoid many age-related diseases. In humans, Parkinson's and Alzheimer's are closely correlated with increased caloric intake. I ask my father: Is cutting calories 40 to 50 percent worth the extra years and protection from disease? He treats it as a rhetorical question. Someone might abstain from cheese-cake for 20 years, I point out, then get hit by a bus at 57. "Life," I say, quoting Damon Runyon (one of my father's heroes), "is 6 to 5 against." "I do what I can," he replies, and he isn't joking, "to even those odds."

On the other hand, a major new study of body weight and health risks by the Centers for Disease Control and Prevention and the National Cancer Institute concluded that the very thin (a person with a body mass index below 18.5—for instance, a man who is 6' and weighs 136 pounds or a woman who is 5'6" and weighs 114) run the same risk of early death as the very fat. Very thin people have no reserves to tap if they fall ill. My dad's thin, but he's not that thin.

Vegetarians tend to live longer, healthier lives than meat eaters. The Japanese diet is high in vegetables and soy products. A Japanese person lives 3 years longer, on average, than an American or Briton. (One-quarter of vegetables eaten in America are french fries.) Okinawans consume 80 percent as many calories as the average Japanese does. Okinawa has the highest percentage of centenarians in the world (600 of its 1.3 million people), four times as high as the rest of the world. The Okinawan diet contains large amounts of foods good for longevity, such as tofu, seaweed, and fish. Fish oils, for instance, are rich in omega-3 fatty acids that, compared with the saturated fats found in meats, don't harden as easily and stick less to artery walls—which has a protective effect against heart disease and stroke. My father likes to quote Satchel Paige—whom he once saw pitch—"Avoid fried meats, which angry up the blood."

Early humans apparently had diets containing vegetables, fruits, nuts, and berries, and large quantities of meat that was naturally low in fat. Isolated tribes in remote parts of the world still eat a Paleolithic diet. A 2002 study of diet, fitness, and disease compared 58 traditional societies with industrialized populations: hunter-gatherers suffer less cardiovascular disease and cancer than people living in "developed" nations; the more your diet diverges from that of hunter-gatherers, the worse your health is likely to be. The contemporary American diet contains twice the fat and one-third the protein of diets maintained by indigenous populations. When you eat animal fats and processed sugar, you increase your risk of disease. When you eat soybeans, cooked tomatoes, and fiber, you reduce your risk of, respectively, breast cancer, prostate cancer, and colon cancer. The major diseases in the industrialized world are caused by departures from the diet to which our early ancestors were adapted.

There's a direct relationship between the percentage of fat in your diet and your risk of cancer. The average Chinese diet contains less than 15 percent fat. The average American diet contains 39 percent fat. The average Chinese has a cholesterol level of 127, compared to 212 for the average American. China has very low rates of heart disease, colon cancer, breast cancer, prostate cancer, or ovarian cancer. What little heart disease and cancer that do exist in China are found overwhelmingly in those regions where people eat the highest amount of fat and cholesterol.

Taoists developed diets that would starve "evil beings"—the Three Worms—which were thought to inhabit the body and hasten its demise by causing disease. Battling the evil beings took the form of denying them the grains, such as wheat and rice, thought to be responsible for their existence, and eating magical foods such as licorice, cinnamon, and ginseng that would kill them. Other approved medicines included herbs, roots, minerals, and animal and plant products such as eggs, turtles, peaches, and parts of trees.

If you want to live longer, you should—in addition to the obvious: eating less and losing weight—move to the country, not take work home, do what you enjoy and feel good about yourself, get a pet, learn to relax, live in the moment, laugh, listen to music, sleep 6 to 7 hours a night; be blessed with long-lived parents and grandparents (35 percent of your longevity is due to genetic factors); be married, hug, hold hands, have sex regularly, have a lot of children, get along with your mother, accept your children, nurture your grandchildren; be well-educated, stimulate your brain, learn new things; be optimistic, channel your anger in a positive way, not always have to be right; not smoke; use less salt, have chocolate occasionally, eat a Mediterranean diet of fruits, vegetables, olive oil, fish, and poultry, drink green tea and moderate amounts of red wine; exercise; have goals, take risks; confide in a friend, not be afraid to seek psychological counseling; be a volunteer, have a role in the community; attend church, find God. (My dad's scorecard: 38 of 42.)

Researchers studied a group of people, ages 66 to 101, who had outlived their siblings by an average of 7 years. One personality characteristic stood out: the longer-lived sibling had a "better sense of humor." My father can, or at least used to be able to (over the last few years, he's almost entirely lost his sense of humor), put hilarious spin on language, hold a room rapt with a story, and tell jokes better than anybody; in the '40s and '50s, he supposedly got invited to the most exclusive Industry parties in Beverly Hills for the solitary purpose of telling Yiddish jokes. On average, married people outlive single people (here's a shocker: the benefit for married men is greater); older siblings outlive younger ones; mothers outlive childless women (by a slight margin); people with higher education live 6 years longer than high school dropouts; Oscar winners outlive unsuccessful nominees by 4 years; CEOs outlive corporate vice presidents; religious people outlive atheists; tall people (men over 6'; women over 5'7") outlive short people by 3 years; nonsmokers live 10 years longer than smokers; thin people live 7 years longer than obese people; American immigrants live 3 years longer than natives; Japanese have the longest life expectancy (82) and Zambians have the briefest (33). Centenarians tend to be assertive, suspicious, and practical. Natalie's former day-care teacher, now a manager for the outpatient clinic of a cancer-care center, says, "It's the assholes who always get better." My father isn't an asshole, but he is mightily self-involved (more self-involved than anyone else?— maybe he simply masks it less well), which seems to have had no ill effects whatsoever on his health or longevity.

Gavin Polone, a 44-year-old television and movie producer/agent, works 6-day weeks and 18-hour days and has rejected marriage and children as antiquated nuisances. Polone views kids as unpredictable clutter that lead to "personal drama." His girlfriend, Elizabeth Oreck, who's 43, says, "People often have children to fulfill some kind of twisted, egocentric reflection of themselves. The truth is, we both prefer animals to people." Polone and Oreck have three dogs and five cats, all rescued from animal shelters or the neighborhood (the mean streets of Beverly Hills). Polone arises at 4:45 A.M., has a waking pulse of 48, eats 8 ounces of dry cereal and drinks 32 ounces of cold green tea for breakfast, and subsists on 1,800 calories a day, primarily protein powder and egg whites. He's 6'1" and weighs 160 pounds. One of his clients, Conan O'Brien, says, "When I met Gavin, he was an assistant to an agent. In time, he became an agent, then a manager. Now he's a producer/bodybuilder/race-car driver. In nine weeks I think he'll be in the space program. I really do. He's evolving into some kind of superbeing. Or a great Bond villain. Whenever I talk to him, I picture him making demands on a big video screen to the United Nations." By consuming less food, Polone hopes to reduce the physical stress that causes aging, extending his life indefinitely. Another client, the director Jon Turteltaub, says about Polone, "He believes that by being really skinny he'll live long enough for stem-cell research to catch up and create new organs for him, and then he can live for eternity."

The Gerontology Research Group—a loose organization of demographers, gerontologists, and epidemiologists who study very old age—believes there's an invisible barrier at age 115. There are only 12 undisputed cases of people ever reaching 115. Very few people who reach age 114 reach 115; since 2001, a dozen 114-year-olds have died before turning 115. Right now there are, according to the GRG, 55 women and 6 men over age 110 worldwide. The oldest age ever reached was 122, in 1997, by a French woman. No matter how little you eat, how much you exercise, and how healthily you live, you apparently can't live longer than 125 years. In 5,000 years of recorded history, there's been no change in the maximum life span. Lucretius, who died in 55 B.C., wrote:

> *Man, by living on, fulfill*
> *As many generations as thou may*
> *Eternal death shall be waiting still*
> *And he who died with light of yesterday*
> *Shall be no briefer time in death's no-more*
> *Than he who perished months or years before.*

How to Live Forever (ii)

There are now thousands of people worldwide in the "longevity movement" who believe it's possible to live for hundreds of years, perhaps forever. Very nearly everyone in the longevity movement is male (my father often has some of their literature lying around). Because they give birth, women seem to feel far less craving for personal immortality.

Ray Kurzweil, who has won a National Medal of Technology award, been inducted into the National Inventors Hall of Fame, is the author of *Fantastic Voyage: Live Long Enough to Live Forever*, and has been working on the problem of artificial intelligence since he was a teenager in the '60s, believes that human immortality is no more than 20 years away. (Even my father acknowledges he's probably not going to be around for that event.) To make sure he lives long enough in order to be around, first, for the biotech revolution, when we'll be able to control how our genes express themselves and ultimately change the genes; and, second, for nanotechnology and the artificial-intelligence revolution, Kurzweil takes 250 supplements a day, drinks 10 glasses of alkaline water and 10 cups of green tea a day, and periodically tracks 40 to 50 fitness indicators, including "tactile sensitivity." Kurzweil makes my dad seem like—as he would say—"a piker."

Millions of robots—"nanobots" the size of blood cells—will keep people forever young by swarming through the body, repairing bones, muscles, arteries, and brain cells. These nanobots will work like repaving crews in our bloodstreams and brains, destroying diseases, rebuilding organs, and obliterating known limits on the human intellect. Improvements to genetic coding will be downloaded from the internet. You won't need a heart.

Kurzweil says, "No more than a hundred genes are involved in the aging process. By manipulating these genes, radical life extension has already been achieved in simpler animals. We are not another animal, subject to nature's whim. Biological evolution passed the baton of progress to human cultural and technological development." He also says that all 30,000 of our genes "are little software programs." We'll be able to block disease-causing genes and introduce new ones that would slow or stop the aging process.

"Life is chemistry," says Brian Wowk, a physicist with 21st Century Medicine. "When the chemistry of life is preserved, so is life."

Aubrey de Grey, a geneticist at the University of Cambridge, says, "In principle, a copy of a living person's brain—all trillion cells of it—could be constructed from scratch, purely by *in vitro* manipulation of neurons into a synaptic network previously scanned from that brain."

João Pedro de Magalhães, a research fellow in genetics at Harvard Medical School, says, "Aging is a sexually transmitted disease that can be defined as a number of time-dependent changes in the body that lead to discomfort, pain, and eventually death. Maybe our grandchildren will be born without aging."

Robert Freitas Jr., a senior research fellow at the Institute for Molecular Manufacturing, says, "Using annual checkups and cleanouts, and some occasional major repairs, your biological age could be restored once a year to the more or less constant physiological age that you select. I see little reason not to go for optimal youth, though trying to maintain your body at the ideal physiological age of ten years old might be difficult and undesirable for other reasons. A rollback to the robust physiology of your late teens or early twenties would be easier to maintain and much more fun." Tee-hee. "That would push your expected age of death up to around 700 to 900 calendar years. You might still eventually die of accidental causes, but you'll live ten times longer than we do now.

"How far can we go with this? If we can eliminate 99 percent of all medically preventable conditions that lead to natural death, your healthy life span, or health span, should increase to about 1,100 years. It may be that you'll find it hard to coax more than a millennium or two out of your original biological body, because deaths from suicides and accidents have remained stubbornly high for the last 100 years, falling by only one third during that time. But our final victory over the scourge of natural death, which we shall achieve later in this century, should extend the health spans of normal human beings by at least tenfold beyond its current maximum length."

Would life get intolerably boring if you lived for a couple of millennia? In the first century B.C., Pliny the Elder, the Roman encyclopedist, wrote of people in previous times who, exhausted by life at age 800, leaped into the sea.

My father now, at 97, seems bored beyond belief—virtually

without a single interest or enthusiasm other than continued existence, day after day after day. In *The Body in Pain*, Elaine Scarry says, "As the body breaks down, it becomes increasingly the object of attention, usurping the place of all other objects, so that finally, in very, very old and sick people, the world may exist only in a circle two feet out from themselves; the exclusive content of perception and speech may become what was eaten, the problems of excreting, the progress of pains, the comfort or discomfort of a particular chair or bed." This is what is suddenly happening to my dad, who until the past few months had still been exercising as if in preparation for a geezers' Ironman competition.

Marc Geddes, a New Zealand writer on artificial intelligence and mathematics, suggests the possibility of "brain refresher drugs," which will prevent "brains from becoming too inflexible. The people living in the far future might be able to alter their bodies and personalities as easily as the people of today change their clothes. The fact that some people living today get tired of life is more likely to be a practical, biological problem than a philosophical one."

Sherwin Nuland, the author of *How We Die*, says about Kurzweil and his fellow fantasists, "They've forgotten that they're acting on the basic biological fear of death and extinction, and it distorts their rational approach to the human condition."

Exhibit A: Leonard Hayflick, professor of anatomy at University of California–San Francisco, a couple of whose public lectures my father has attended, explains that every chromosome has tails at its end that get shorter as a cell divides. Over time, these tails, called telomeres, become so short that their function is disrupted, and this, in turn, leads the cell to stop proliferating. Average telomere length, therefore, gives some

indication of how many divisions the cell has already under-
gone and how many remain before it can no longer replicate.
I.e., there's an intrinsic limit to how long humans can live.

In Tennyson's *Tithonus*, the eponymous protagonist, who is
granted his wish of immortality without realizing he'd be aging
forever, decides he wants to die:

> . . . *Let me go: take back thy gift.*
> *Why should a man desire in any way*
> *To vary from the kindly race of men,*
> *Or pass beyond the goal of ordinance*
> *Where all should pause, as is most meet for all?*
> *Release me, and restore me to the ground.*

My father doesn't see it like that. Good for him.

Last Words

Leonard Bernstein said, "What's this?"

Babe Ruth said, "I'm going over the valley."

Cotton Mather said, "Is this all? Is this what I feared when I prayed against a hard death? Oh, I can bear this. I can bear it!"

The Greek philosopher Anaxarchus, pounded to death with pestles in the fourth century B.C., said, "Pound, pound the pouch containing Anaxarchus. You pound not Anaxarchus."

Air Force Major Norman Basell, flying bandleader Glenn Miller to France on a flight that vanished over the English Channel, said, "What's the matter, Miller—do you want to live forever?"

The philologist Barthold George Niebuhr, noticing that his medicine was intended only for terminal cases, asked, "What essential substance is this? Am I so far gone?"

Angelica Kauffmann, an eighteenth-century artist, stopped her cousin—who had begun to read her a hymn for the dying—and said, "No, Johann, I will not hear that. Read me the 'Hymn for the Sick' on page 128."

William H. Vanderbilt, president of the New York Central Railroad, said, in 1885, "I have no real gratification or enjoyment of any sort more than my neighbor down the block who is worth only half a million."

Frederick the Great, King of Prussia, said, "I am tired of ruling over slaves."

Louise, Queen of Prussia, said, "I am a queen, but I have no power to move my arms."

Queen Elizabeth I said, "All my possessions for one moment of time."

Phillip III, king of Spain, said, "Oh would to God I had never reigned. Oh that those years in my kingdom I had lived a solitary life in the wilderness. Oh that I had lived alone with God. How much more secure should I have died. With how much more confidence should I have gone to the throne of God. What doth all my glory profit but that I have so much the more torment in my death?"

Cardinal Henry Beaufort said, "Will not all my riches save me? What, is there no bribing death?"

Henry James said, "So here it is at last, the distinguished thing."

Anne Boleyn said, "The executioner is, I believe, an expert, and my neck is very slender."

Marie Antoinette, tripping over her executioner's foot, said, "Monsieur, I beg your pardon. I did not do it on purpose."

Charles II said, "I have been a most unconscionable time dying, but I beg you to excuse it."

Sir William Davenant, seventeenth-century British Poet Laureate, unable to complete a final poem, said, "I shall have to ask leave to desist, when I am interrupted by so great an experiment as dying."

Rabelais said, "I am going in search of a great perhaps."

James Thurber said, "God bless. God damn."

H. G. Wells said, "God damn you all; I told you so."

Francis Buckland, an inspector of fisheries, said, "God is so good to the little fishes, I do not believe He would let their inspector suffer shipwreck at last."

Eugène Ysaÿe, a Belgian violinist and composer, said, after his Fourth Sonata was played for him, "Splendid. The finale just a little too fast."

James Quin, an eighteenth-century British actor, said, "I could wish this tragic scene were over, but I hope to go through it with becoming modesty."

Replying to the observation that dying must be very hard, the actor Edmund Gwenn said, "It is. But not as hard as farce."

Flo Ziegfeld said, "Curtain! Fast music! Light! Ready for the finale! Great! The show looks good! The show looks good!"

James Croll, a lifelong teetotaler, said, "I'll take a wee drop of that. I don't think there's much fear of me learning to drink now."

The eighteenth-century sociologist Auguste Comte said, "What an irreparable loss!"

Da Vinci said, "I have offended God and mankind because my work did not reach the quality it should have."

The British newspaper tycoon Lord Beaverbrook said, "This is my final word. It is time for me to become an apprentice once more. I have not settled in which direction."

Machiavelli said, "I desire to go to hell and not heaven. In the former place I shall enjoy the company of popes, kings, and princes, while in the latter are only beggars, monks, and apostles."

Looking at a lamp that flared at his bedside, Voltaire said, "The flames already?"

Kansas City Chiefs running back Stone Johnson, killed in a

football game, said, "Oh my God, oh my God! Where's my head? Where's my head?"

The American Civil War commander General John Sedgwick, who was killed at the battle of Spotsylvania in 1864, looked over a parapet at the Confederate troops and said, "They couldn't hit an elephant at this dist—"

Vicomte de Turenne, a French soldier killed at the battle of Sasbach in 1675, said, "I did not mean to be killed today."

Initially, the rope broke when the Russian revolutionary Bestoujeff was hanged; "Nothing succeeds with me," he said. "Even here I meet with disappointment."

Joseph II, Holy Roman Emperor, said, "Let my epitaph be, 'Here lies Joseph, who was unsuccessful in all his undertakings.'"

Nicholas Boileau, a French critic, responding to a playwright who asked Boileau to read his new play, said, "Do you wish to hasten my last hour?"

Oscar Wilde, dying in a tacky Paris hotel, said, "My wallpaper and I are fighting a duel to the death. One or the other of us has to go."

Charles d'Evereruard, a gourmet, was asked by his confessor if he would be reconciled with Christ; d'Evereruard replied, "With all my heart I would fain be reconciled with my stomach, which no longer performs its usual functions."

Frédéric Moyse, guillotined for killing his own son, said, "What, would you execute the father of a family?"

Longfellow said to his sister, "Now I know I must be very ill, since you have been sent for."

George Fordyce, a physician, told his daughter, who had been reading to him, "Stop. Go out of the room. I am about to die."

Baron Georges Cuvier, a zoologist, said to his daughter,

who was drinking a glass of lemonade he had refused, "It is delightful to see those whom I love still able to swallow."

O. O. McIntyre, an American newspaper columnist, said to his wife, "Snooks, will you please turn this way? I like to look at your face."

Lady Astor, the first woman member of British Parliament, surrounded by her entire family on her deathbed, said, "Am I dying, or is this my birthday?"

Goethe said, "More light."

The Indian chief Crowfoot said, "A little while and I will be gone from you. Whither I cannot tell. From nowhere we come, into nowhere we go. What is life? It is the flash of a firefly in the night. It is the breath of a buffalo in the wintertime. It is the little shadow which runs across the grass and loses itself in the sunset."

Buddha said, "Decay is inherent in all things."

Gertrude Stein asked Alice B. Toklas, "What is the answer?" When Toklas didn't respond, Stein laughed and said, "In that case, what is the question?"

After finishing a poem on New Year's Eve about New Year's Day, Johann Georg Jacobi said, "I shall not in fact see the New Year which I have just commemorated."

Andrew Bradford, the publisher of Philadelphia's first newspaper, said, "Oh Lord, forgive the errata!"

Dominique Bouhours, a seventeenth-century French Jesuit who was the leading grammarian of his day, said, "I am about to—or I am going to—die; either expression is used."

Replying to a question about whether he was in pain, Henry Prince of Wales, son of James I, said, "I would say 'somewhat,' but I cannot utter it."

Karl Marx, asked by his housekeeper if he had a last message for the world, said, "Go on, get out. Last words are for fools who haven't said enough."

Pancho Villa said, "Don't let it end like this. Tell them I said something."

"In the event of my death," my mother's will said, "I would like to have my body cremated and the ashes disposed of in the simplest way possible. My first choice would have been to donate my heart, kidneys, and cornea for transplants. However, it is not possible to donate the organs of someone with cancer. I realize that cremation is not in accordance with Jewish law, but I think it is the most sensible method of disposing of a lifeless body. Although I do not want a religious memorial service, I hope it is helpful to family and friends to have an informal gathering of people, so that each may draw strength from one another. I leave this world without regrets or bitterness of any kind. I have had a good life. May the future be kind to each of you. Shalom." Her equanimity in the face of mortality.

What will be my father's last words?

What will be mine?

Bloodline to Star Power (iii)

In the early 1970s, my half sister, Emily, was working as a maid at a motel in Oregon. "Don't know how it happened," my father explained, "but Pepi and his wife were guests at this posh place." Emily introduced herself, told him who she was, and Schildkraut gave her one of his "stylish Borsalino felt hats, which he wore in rakish over-one-eye European style—always the matinee idol—as a souvenir." She gave the hat to my father, who "had it in the closet for years, but it must have got thrown out when I moved after your mother's death."

I tell this story to Emily, who writes back, "Concerning the story about Joseph Schildkraut giving me a hat: that's a total mystery to me! I did work for a short time in a hotel in Cannon Beach, Oregon. I have no memory of this mysterious visitor— or even seeing him—except in the movie *The Diary of Anne Frank*. Either I was that spaced-out in those days and have blocked out this significant event, or once again our Pop has fabricated another yarn for you from his rich imagination. Sorry."

I relay what Emily has said back to my father, who wants to know: "Then where did the Borsalino hat come from? I distinctly remember Emily telling us that when she learned

Joseph was a guest at the Oregon resort she was working at, she went over to him, told him her father's original name, they talked for a few minutes, and then Pepi gave her the hat. He wore hats like a Borsalino in his stage and screen roles back in the days when all male actors wore hats. And Borsalino, an expensive Italian-made hat, would be his style."

Then, shortly afterward, in a truly weird coincidence, an old friend of our family's calls my father and asks him to pick up two boxes of odds and ends that my father had left with them many years ago. "The lid flipped open on one of the boxes, and on top there was the hat Schildkraut gave to Emily at that Oregon coast resort back in the early '70s. Thought you'd be interested to learn about my (accidental) archaeological finding."

I am, I am, but the hat proves nothing. Only very recently I happened to discover that Schildkraut died in 1964, which means that Emily—sweetly seeking my father's appreciation—must have invented the entire story, my father invented the story, I've got the details wrong, or being in a family is indistinguishable from playing telephone. And yet the photograph in *My Father and I* of Schildkraut kissing Susan Strasberg on the forehead in *The Diary of Anne Frank* mimics exactly the melodramatic bad acting in two photographs of my father kissing Emily when she was very little. In so many photographs of "Pepi" or my father or me is this certain quality of mugging hungrily, of pretty-boyness (me till I was 12, my father into late middle age, Schildkraut until he was dead), of stilted posedness, of on-your-knees-before-the-camera obsequiousness, of needing to be liked by the lens, of peasant smilingness, of overreliance upon previous modes of appearing in pictures . . .

Schildkraut also has what is to me a disturbing-because-familiar detachment toward his own feelings. "Maybe there was no such thing as love in real life," he writes. "These all-consuming agonies and ecstasies of love existed only on the stage." I once wrote about stuttering that "it prevents you from ever entirely losing self-consciousness when expressing such traditional and truly important emotions as love, hate, joy, and deep pain. Always first aware not of the naked feeling itself but of the best way to phrase the feeling so as to avoid verbal repetition, you come to think of emotions as belonging to other people, being the world's happy property and not yours—not really yours except by way of disingenuous circumlocution."

The tightest warp and woof I can weave comes from the sound of the syntax. Joseph says of Rudolph, "He was passionately in love with the sound of words. They intoxicated him." Joseph says of his mother, "She had an acute business sense, a talent for making every kreuzer count." My father says, "You can bet all the borscht in Brownsville on that." My father writes, "It's been at least a year since that coffee-klatch-cum-current-events-discussion-group held its final meeting, but many people at Woodlake still talk about the explosive events of that fateful day." I write, "The tightest warp and woof I can weave comes from the sound of the syntax." Do you hear the keynote—the incessant buzz and hum of alliteration? I point out to my father what I see as the link between Schildkraut's alliteration-dependent writing style, my father's style, and my own (as well as my stutter), and he writes back, "About Joseph Schildkraut's style: I believe the book he wrote in collaboration [*My Father and I*, "as told to Leo Lania"] is the only thing he's ever written. Solo, or with somebody's help. Don't know how much his collaborator did and what Pepi contributed. My style? Strictly journalese. Marked—riddled?—by too much, far too much, alliteration. The O. Henry influence: as a young boy of 7 or 8, I read his stories over and over. My brother Phil had won a complete set of O. Henry in a writing contest and there they were for me to devour—and (sadly) to incorporate, lock, stock, and barrel, into my own writing."

A decade ago I told my father that I hoped to travel someday to Eastern Europe to trace the Schildkraut ancestry, and he responded, "That would be a dream trip—the two of us investigating the Schildkraut strain in Austria, Germany, and the Ukraine. Whenever you're ready, I'll be ready. It would be a great adventure." (We've never gone.) I explained that what I'm most interested in is my need to get him to tell the stories over and over and over again and his ceaseless capacity to reinvent and extend the material. He replied (and this is what I've come to recognize as my father's signature and see projected forward in myself and backward in Schildkraut: an unshakable self-consciousness), "Writing about it, you'll probably use and exploit how I arrogated to myself the 'cousins, yeah, they're probably second cousins' relationship. And how I told and retold—dined out a lot on it, as the saying goes—the story of my one actual involvement, in person, with Pepi: the Einstein memorial night, etc."

Well, so, as my father likes to say, what? What is this correlation-seeking but a ghoulish attempt to backform a bloodline to star power? What proof is it, in any case, to find common traits in a putative relative's memoir? Is he or isn't he? Was he or wasn't he? I don't know, I can't know, and I'll never know; why, then, is it important for me to believe there's a link? Why do I care about being related to someone who—on the basis of my father's stories and *The Diary of Anne Frank*—appears to be a singularly unpleasant human being and painfully ham-fisted actor? Star-fucker: name-dropper: strain-strainer. My father now informs me that he believes—although he can't be absolutely certain—that we're related to Robert

Shields (né Schildkraut), of the former San Francisco mime
duo Shields and Yarnell, and I can't help it: I think, well, then,
maybe I'm also related to Brooke Shields; toward the end of
Endless Love, when she's crying in that dark New York hotel
room, trying to say good-bye to David, and her hair is braided
and rolled up in a bun, she does, it seems to me, especially in
the mouth and chin area, look at least a little the way I sometimes looked as a teenager.

Sex and Death (iv)

In 1986, Denys Arcand released his movie *The Decline of the American Empire*, an obsessive talkathon on the subject of sex. Seventeen years later, the sequel appeared—*The Barbarian Invasions*, an obsessive talkathon on the subject of death. The film about sex is called *Decline*. The film about death is called *Invasions*. A point is being made here:

When groups of verve monkeys feed, several males sit with their backs to the group and brandish their genitals to ward off potential scavengers. If an unknown animal approaches, male verves get an erection and make a threatening face. Fighter pilots, when escaping dangerous situations, release extremely high levels of epinephrine (the hormone released by stress) and sometimes ejaculate.

Louis Réard, a French auto engineer who also ran his mother's lingerie business, designed a two-piece swimsuit. Four days before he presented the swimsuit to the public, the U.S. military exploded a nuclear device near a group of small islands in the Pacific known as the Bikini atoll. On July 5, 1946, Réard unveiled the swimsuit and claimed the bikini was named for the beauty of the islands rather than for the atomic blast.

Men who are hanged sometimes have erections and orgasms,

which are caused by the snapping of the spinal cord; when the nerves beneath the neck are severed from the spine, the spasm can create a mechanical, reflexive ejaculation. An engraving by Daumier shows a torture chamber filled with skeletons in chains and a hanged man ejaculating. In Marquis de Sade's *Justine*, Thérèse helps Roland achieve orgasm by briefly hanging him; afterward, he exclaims, "Oh, Thérèse! Oh, those feelings are indescribable. They exceed everything!" In *Ulysses*, the Croppy Boy "gives up the ghost. A violent erection of the hanged sends gouts of sperm spouting through his dead clothes on to the cobblestones. Mrs. Bellingham, Mrs. Yelverton Barry, and the Honourable Mrs. Mervyn Talboys rush forward with their handkerchiefs to sop it up." Pathologist Sir Bernard Spilsbury's handwritten autopsy note of an early twentieth-century hanging states that there was no "seminal effusion" on this occasion, which implies that it often occurred on other occasions. *Spilsbury*. The photograph of the execution of the Lincoln conspirators in 1865 shows one of the men, Lewis Powell, with an erection after he was hanged.

James Boswell frequently attended public hangings in eighteenth-century London. Afterward, he liked to look at the faces of the dead bodies. Once, while the bodies were still dangling, he went directly to a prostitute. "I have got a shocking sight in my head," he said he told her. "Take it out."

Easier said than done, because, as Michel Houellebecq writes in *Elementary Particles*, "The chromosomal separation at the moment of meiosis which creates haploid gametes is in itself a source of structural instability. In other words, all species dependent on sexual reproduction are by definition mortal."

In *The Merchant and the Friar*, the nineteenth-century poet and critic Sir Francis Palgrave wrote, "Coeval with the first pulsation, when the fibers quiver, and the organs quicken into vitality, is the germ of death. Before our members are fashioned is the narrow grave dug, in which they are to be entombed."

Jules Bordet, a Belgian scientist, wrote, in a famous formulation 100 years ago, "Life is the maintenance of an equilibrium that is perpetually threatened."

"Boys are like Pez dispensers," says a teenage girl. "Show 'em a nipple and they get an erection."

In *The Tragic Sense of Life*, Miguel de Unamuno wrote, "To live is to give oneself, perpetuate oneself, and to perpetuate oneself, to give oneself, is to die. Perhaps the supreme delight of procreation is nothing other than a foretasting or savoring of death, the spilling of one's own vital essence. We unite with another, but it is to divide ourselves: that most intimate embrace is naught but a most intimate uprooting. In essence, the delight of sexual love, the genetic spasm, is a sensation of resurrection, of resuscitation in another, for only in others can we resuscitate and perpetuate ourselves."

A male American college student says, "I picture Death as being millions of years old but only looking about forty."

"Life," Virginia Woolf wrote in her diary when she was 44, "is, as I've said since I was 10, awfully interesting—if anything, quicker, keener at 44 than 24, more desperate, I suppose, as the river shoots to Niagara—my new vision of death; active, positive, like all the rest, exciting; & of great importance—as an experience."

Giacomo Leopardi wrote, "Death is not an evil, for it liberates from all evils, and if it deprives man of any good thing, it also takes away his desire for it. Old age is the supreme evil, for it deprives man of all pleasures, while leaving his appetite for them, and brings with it all sufferings. Nevertheless, men fear death and desire old age."

Tom Stoppard: "Age is a high price to pay for maturity."

Antony says to Cleopatra, "I am dying, Egypt, dying."

According to Thomas Browne, the physician and author of *Religio Medici*, "The long habit of living indisposeth us to dying."

When Confucius realized he was about to die, he wept.

All human beings have bodies. All bodies are mortal. Yours, too, is one of these bodies.

In World War II, my father was assigned to Army Information and Education; his job was to lecture to the troops about America's allies and enemies and send news releases to the hometown newspapers of the men in the outfit. If a private was promoted to Private First Class, my father would send a press release to the private's hometown paper announcing that he'd been promoted for his "courage under fire" and "military bearing." But when the radio battalion headquarters in the middle of the compound on Okinawa announced, on August 8, 1945, that the Japanese had surrendered unconditionally and would be signing the peace treaty later that day aboard ship in Tokyo Bay, my father went berserk and raced down to the mess hall, where he told the mess sergeant, Coleman Peterson, that he was taking over and would be serving breakfast to the 120 men in the unit.

Sergeant Peterson told my father he'd lost his mind and would want to quit after the first six grunts went through the chow line complaining that the scrambled eggs were too hard and the pancakes were too thin. My dad told Peterson nobody, including Douglas MacArthur, was going to stop him.

Peterson insisted on at least preparing the egg and pancake mixes. My father agreed, tied an apron around his waist, and when the first man came through the line, asking what was on the menu this morning, my father sang out, "Horseshit on French toast. No, actually, the V-J Day special: scrambled eggs, bacon, all the pancakes you can eat, and the strongest coffee on the island!"

Apparently, though, my father is not immortal:

On my most recent visit, he evaluated, as he always does, what kind of physical shape I seemed to be in and contemplated, as he always does, the potential safety hazards of my one-handed driving. He asked me, as he always did, whether Natalie had enrolled in swimming lessons yet—he was concerned that she'd wander into Lake Washington and drown—and when we went to a department store so he could buy a birthday present for Natalie, he made sure, as he always did, that I paid for it. He apparently wants to take his not very vast fortune with him.

The next morning, when I arrived 15 minutes late to take him out to brunch, he was sobbing. Fearful that I'd perished in an auto accident, he'd called my hotel, 911, and even Laurie back in Seattle to see if she'd heard anything about my whereabouts. At the restaurant, he vehemently criticized the spiciness of the soup, which couldn't have been more bland; he wanted nothing sharp to throw him off stride.

Having not seen my father for several months, I was startled by his swift decline: he shuffled around his tiny apartment, which was almost empty, because of his new fixation with getting rid of nearly everything he owned; his breathing was loud and labored; his eyes were glassy and flat; a pouch of skin sagged beneath his left eye; a portion of his left ear had been excised in surgery to remove skin cancer; he ping-ponged back and forth between diarrhea and constipation; he often neglected to zip his zipper.

Waiting for *Sicko* to start, he asked me when and where I learned the facts of life. The people in the row behind us convulsed into giggles, and though it seemed a little late to be discussing the birds 'n' the bees, I had to answer quite loudly—his hearing aid wasn't working well—that I consulted a variety of sources on the subject. Thanks to his malfunctioning hearing aid, he found the movie utterly unintelligible. Leaving the theater before the lights had come up, he took a bad tumble down the stairs, to the collective gasp of the audience.

"I'm perpetually tired," he wrote me when I returned home. "Used to be—until a year ago—I could swim a dozen laps. Can just about make 3 to 4 now. I crave sleep a lot. With the aid of sleeping tablets—Tylenol PM—I sleep in two sessions, from 9:30 to 4:30, then breakfast, then back to bed for a couple of hours, plus an occasional nap of one-hour duration. I used to go to the 18-hole putting green at Woodlake often, now indifferent to its lure. Haven't gone in a couple of months. On the positive side, I still work out in the gym for 30 minutes. Usually on the stationary bike. Do that after lunch. Like a forced march. But I still do it and am glad I've still got the willpower. To sum it up, some of my most vexing problems are traceable, I'm sure—and so are you and you're correct—to the passages of the years. Ninety-seven ain't 79." For my father, this very partial and begrudging acknowledgment constitutes a major declension.

The Story Told One Last Time, from Beginning to End

As soon as your reproductive role has been accomplished, you're disposable.

After sexual maturation, deterioration in peak efficiency occurs because, as Harold Morowitz, a professor of biology at George Mason University, says, "perfect order requires infinite work." Also, deterioration builds on itself.

In the late nineteenth century, August Weismann, a German biologist, made a distinction between "the immortality of reproductive cells, the cells in the body that carry genes forward to the next generation, and the mortality of the rest, which will age and die." Death takes place, he said, "because a worn-out tissue cannot forever renew itself, and because a capacity for increase by means of cell-division is not everlasting but finite."

Once a body's mission is accomplished, nature has little interest in what happens next. Reproductive life spans of members of a species work as perfectly as possible to match the time an individual of that species might expect to survive before dying. In other words, physiological resources go into reproduction, not into prolonging life thereafter.

The force of natural selection declines with age. Natural

selection has shaped human biology in such a way that aging and death become increasingly likely by the time you reach your 40s. If a disaster strikes a person who has passed the age of reproductive fitness, the consequences are by and large unimportant to the survival of the rest of the species.

Nature favors the accumulation of genes that do beneficial things early in life, even though they might do harmful things late in life, since—under normal conditions—most animals do not live long enough for the harmful effects to cause a problem. The same general mechanism that protects against cancer protects against aging. Long-lived species, with their better cellular protection, get cancer later than short-lived species.

The pineal gland is your internal clock. It knows how old you are, and it knows when you're past your reproductive prime. As soon as it senses that you're too old to reproduce effectively—around age 45—it begins to produce far lower levels of melatonin, which signals all of your other systems to break down and the aging process to begin. (Women's larger pineal gland is another reason why women age more slowly than men, and it may be why they live longer.)

These low levels of melatonin cause, for instance, your immune system to shut down and your endocrine system to produce fewer sex hormones. Lower levels of sex hormones in turn lead to the atrophy of sexual organs in both men and women, to a decrease as well in sexual interest and the ability to perform. At 90, my father's equipment finally quit.

In the late stages of adulthood, moths mimic the movements of juvenile moths, leading predators away from young moths and sacrificing their own lives, in order to benefit the species. What I've been trying to get to all along, in a way, is this: The individual doesn't matter. You, Dad, in the large scheme of things, don't matter. I, Dad, don't matter. We're vectors on the grids of cellular life. We carry 10 to 12 genes with mutations that are potentially lethal. These mutations are passed on to our children—you to me, me to Natalie. Aging followed by death is the price we pay for the immortality of our genes. You find this information soul-killing; I find it thrilling, liberating. Life, in my view, is simple, tragic, and eerily beautiful.

Exit Interviews

Asked what the meaning of life is, the paleontologist Stephen Jay Gould said, "We are here because one odd group of fishes had a peculiar fin anatomy that could transform into legs for terrestrial creatures; because comets struck the earth and wiped out the dinosaurs, thereby giving mammals a chance not otherwise available; because the earth never froze entirely during an ice age; because a small and tenuous species, arising in Africa a quarter of a million years ago, has managed, so far, to survive by hook and by crook. We may yearn for a 'higher' answer, but none exists." (Darwin on Darwinism: "There is grandeur in this view of life." Stoppard on evolution: "I've always thought the idea of God is absolutely preposterous, but slightly more plausible than the alternative proposition that, given enough time, some green slime could write Shakespeare's sonnets.")

Robert Wilkoske, who owns a wrecking company in Cheyenne, Wyoming, said, "Animals will fight to the death to try to survive. Even if it's a rattlesnake swallowing a gopher. The gopher tries to get away, but after the snake gets ahold of him, he's going down. That's the way it is with a human, too. I've seen animals fight, I've seen animals fight when the odds were against them. They know they're going to get whipped, but they'll fight to the death to try to stay alive. It isn't any particular thing we're living for, just the instinct to stay alive. But I'm no authority."

José Martinez, a taxi driver, said, "We're here to die, just live and die. I do some fishing, take my girl out, pay taxes, do a little reading, then get ready to drop dead. You're here or you're gone. You're like the wind. After you're gone, other people will come. We're gonna destroy ourselves, nothing we can do about it. It's too late to make it better. You've got to be strong about it. The only cure for the world's illness is nuclear war. Wipe everything out and start over."

Woody Allen: "We are adrift, alone in the cosmos, wreaking monstrous violence on one another out of frustration and pain." No punch line.

Wilfred Beckerman, a British economist, said, "The chances of mankind turning out to be more than just a blip in the process of evolution are very small."

The rapper Ice-T said, "We're here to stick our heads above the water for just a minute, look around, and go back under. A human being is just another animal in the big jungle. We have a lot of different instincts, and they're all animal. We kill because we're angry or need food. We have babies because it feels good and we want to care for other people. Once you have a kid, you look at the kid and see yourself again. You realize, 'Oh, that's why we're here.' Life is really short and you're going to die, so you should leave someone else to keep his head above the water. Everything else is just passing time until the next generation, setting up shop. Just chill out and reproduce. Keep the species alive."

Nicholas Vislocky, the assistant superintendent of a cemetery, said, "In the beginning, being a gravedigger bothered me.

All you see is the grieving family. You carry the casket. You imagine the person who's in there. And the thing that touches you most is the kids when they pass away. Their caskets are white, for purity, and they're smaller, only like three feet long. They didn't have a chance to experience anything. It's like they were robbed of something. When you see the small white caskets, you appreciate the short, split-second lifetime you have."

Shortly before his 97th birthday, when I asked my father what he's learned over such a long life, he said, "The secret of a long, healthy life is to exercise every day even if it's only for thirty minutes, and don't let anything deter you from it." When I explained that I meant not just how to live a long life but what it all amounted to, if anything, he shrugged and trotted out hoary "truths": "There's one comforting thing about the aging process: I'll never have to do it again." "Dying is easy. The least of us manage that. Living is the trick." "On balance, the world is a much better place than it was in Brooklyn, New York, in 1910." Which—the last—led him to consider what he might have achieved had he stayed in school and gotten his bachelor's degree from CCNY, then a master's in journalism from Columbia; perhaps he would have realized his fantasy: sports columnist for the *New York Times* (à la his hero Red Smith). This led to tears, though, so he cut short the discussion and said, "Let's go for a walk," which we did. He no longer plays tennis or golfs or jogs. He used to say that he could never imagine not being able to do at least five laps around Wood-lake, totaling a little over a mile. Now he could barely shuffle his way around once, interspersed with frequent rests on benches.

As he'd be the first to point out, this could partly be explained by the fact that, after rescheduling his colonoscopy several times, he'd finally had it done a few days before. Complaining all the way home about the "disrespectful" way he felt the nurses had treated him, he was mortified by how thoroughly he'd pissed and shat his gown during the procedure. The results: no cancer, no nothing, only a minor case of diverticulitis, relatively easily remedied, but now he's obsessed and depressed about that (obsession and depression being indistinguishable for him—I've come to realize—from the life force).

Notes for Eulogy for My Father

In the early 1930s, my father worked as a minor-league umpire on the East Coast, teaming up occasionally with Emmett Ashford, who was something of a showman and who thirty years later became the first black umpire in the major leagues. Some people thought all of my father's behind-the-plate antics amounted to little more than "white Ashford." We'd go to Giants games not when Koufax was the competition or bats were being given away but when Ashford was calling balls and strikes. All game long, my dad would keep his binoculars on Ashford and say to me, "Emmett's calling a low strike" or "Emmett was out of position on that one" or "If that guy gives Emmett any more guff, Emmett's going to give him the old heave-ho." Then I'd look up and Emmett would be giving the guy the old heave-ho.

It wasn't the major leagues that played at Golden Gate Park. It wasn't even the minor leagues. It was something called the industrial league. The Machinists would play the Accountants; Pacific Gas and Electric would play Western Airlines. But they played with a hard ball, they played for blood, their wives cheered like enraged schoolgirls, and my father was the umpire. He'd leave on Sunday morning, carrying his spikes and metal mask, with his chest protector underneath his blue uniform and a little whisk broom, with which to dust off home plate, sticking out of his pocket. I'll never forget the first time I saw him umpire.

It wasn't a stadium at all but an immense field without fences. There was a diamond, though, and dugouts and a half-circle of stands. I stood behind the screen, watching Denny's Restaurant play Safeway Market. Neither team meant a thing to me, and after a few innings I looked around for my father, whom I figured must be working the next game. Then I realized the big man in blue, squatting behind the catcher with every pitch, was my dad. In certain sections of the country, in certain leagues and stadiums, the spectators are expected to focus all of their economic and sexual frustrations upon the lonely figure of the umpire, but in San Francisco, in Golden Gate Park, on at least one Sunday in the summer of 1966, they didn't do that.

Denny's Restaurant and Safeway Market weren't playing up to par; my father soon emerged as the main attraction. When a batter took a called third strike, my father would parody the victim's indignation. When a batter drew a walk, my father would run halfway to first base with him to speed things along. He was the only umpire working the game, so on balls hit to the outfield he'd run down the foul line to make sure the ball had been caught, and on balls hit to the infield he'd run to first base to be in position to decide. He signaled safe by spreading his arms and flapping them, as if readying for flight. He signaled out by jerking his thumb, and the entire right side of his body, down. Between innings he juggled three baseballs.

He worked all day, four long games, 10 in the morning until 6 at night, and at the last out of the last game the fans applauded. It was only light, polite, scattered applause, and maybe they were clapping for the winning team, but to me it was a thunderous ovation and they were thanking the umpire. I stood up behind the screen and joined them. I cheered for my father.

Two of the things I love the most in the world—language and sports—my father taught me to love. I'm no longer much of an athlete at all. I have a bad back, tendonitis in my shoulder, a trick knee, I wear orthotics in my shoes to balance the unevenness of my legs, and I have a little pinch in my neck that's been bothering me lately, whereas at 97 my father's major ailment appears to be tennis elbow. He gets upset when it rains because that means he can only work out in the gym rather than walk around the track and then work out in the gym. He still swims most days. Until very recently he played golf and, occasionally, tennis. He's the most vigorous person I've ever known. From his essay about a rafting trip our family took down the Salmon River: "I was up at 6 the next morning and volunteered to gather the kindling and other firewood. The other members of my family snuggled in their sleeping bags and made it just in time for the 7:30 breakfast."

Since I was 6 years old, the first thing he and I have done every morning is read the sports page. One of my fondest memories is from about 20 years ago—the two of us sitting on his couch in the dark, listening to the radio broadcast of a Giants-Dodgers game; when Mike Marshall hit a three-run home run in the 10th inning to win it for the Dodgers, he and I looked at each other and we were both, a little weirdly, crying.

Games have held us together, but also words. I've always loved his love of puns, bad puns and worse puns; admired his ability to tell a joke and a story. The day before my college commencement, he and I went on a tour of John Brown House at the Rhode Island Historical Society. On and on the docent droned, giving us the official version of American history. My father and I tried not to laugh, but as we went from room to room, we were in an ecstasy of impudent giggles. "Subvert the dominant paradigm": so goes the bumper sticker, which has passed now into cultural cliché. In so many ways, though, he has showed me how to do exactly that: to question received wisdom, to insist on my own angle, to view language as a playground, and a playground as bliss. He showed me how to love the words that emerged from my mouth and from my typewriter, how to love being in my own body, how to love being in my own skin and not some other skin.

On an Army transport ship taking my father and 5,000 other soldiers from Seattle to Okinawa in May 1945, my father played in a poker game that continued for three days and nights; players left only to use the bathroom or get food or sleep. They'd all read about the bloody Marine invasion on Okinawa a month before, so there was, according to my father, a fatalistic feeling about the game of "Tomorrow we die" and "Hell, it's only money."

On the third day, my father was ahead $1,000. They were playing Seven-Card Stud. The first two cards he drew were kings. He immediately bet the $2 limit, trying to drive out as many of the other players as he could—a poker strategy his father had taught him. My dad drew a third king on the fourth card, giving him what was now an extremely hard-to-beat hand.

By the fifth card there were only two people left—my dad and a young private from Georgia, "Rebel."

When my father bet $2, Rebel said, "Ah raise you, Sarge. It's two dollars and two dollars better."

My father, figuring that Rebel had maybe a pair or a possible straight, threw in $2 to see him. Another poker lesson learned by my father from his father: never let anybody bluff you, especially when you and the other player are the last two in the game. "You've got to keep them honest," he told him, "even if you have to put in your last dime to 'see' them. Remember that."

On the sixth card, my father began with a bet and Rebel again raised him $2. My dad now had four kings and, looking at the cards Rebel was showing, he couldn't imagine what he might have that would beat four kings. My father "saw" Rebel's raise.

When the seventh card was dealt "down and dirty," my father said, "It's up to the raiser. Up to you, Rebel."

"It'll cost you four dollars to see me, Sarge," he said, which got a laugh from some of his buddies.

My father saw Rebel again and asked him what he had.

"I got me a little old straight," he said and started to rake in the $75 pot.

"Not good enough, Rebel," my father said, showing his four kings.

Rebel slammed his cards down on the table and said, "You play like a Gahdamned Jew!"—stretching the word "Jew" out, according to my father, as if it had several syllables, making it sound like "Jooo-ooo."

The chow whistle sounded, the game broke up, and my father asked Rebel, "Why did you use that expression, 'play like a Goddamned Jew'?"

Rebel said that his father told him that all Jews were sharp poker players. My dad said that some of his friends back in

Brooklyn were poor players, almost as bad as Rebel and his friends. (Whenever my grandfather got good cards, his entire manner would change. He'd pull his chair up closer to the table and say in Yiddish, "Ubber Yetz," which, loosely translated, means "But, now . . .": the battle was joined and my grandfather was ready for action. The other players would laugh and say, "Well, it looks like Sam has one of his 'Ubber Yetz' hands. Who's going to see him?" "Enough with the jokes," he'd say. "Are you here to play poker? I bet a quarter for openers. Is anybody in?" One or two would stay in and my grandfather would usually win the pots, which were never very big.) Then my father told Rebel he was Jewish. Rebel didn't believe him; my father had blue eyes, blond hair, and a deep tan. My dad said that he'd provide proof if he'd just step into the latrine, where he'd show him that he was circumcised. Rebel said he believed him.

The comedian Danny Kaye and my father were classmates at P.S. 149. In the mid-1950s, shortly before I was born, Kaye gave a one-man performance at the Hollywood Bowl, which my father and mother and half a dozen of their friends attended. At intermission, Kaye walked to the front of the stage and asked how many in the audience were from Brooklyn. Quite a few hands went up. He asked how many had gone to P.S. 149. About 10 people raised their hands. Then he asked if anyone remembered the P.S. 149 fight song. My dad's was the only hand still up. Kaye said, "Great, let's do it," and gave the band the beat. My mother tugged at my father's coat, saying, "Milt, you're embarrassing me. Please sit down." My parents' friends urged my mother to relax. Danny Kaye and my father sang their alma mater's fight song:

149 is the school for me
Drives away all adversity
Steady and true
We'll be to you
Loyal to 149
RAH RAH
Raise on high
The red and white
Cheer it
With all your might
Loyal all to 149.

The crowd went crazy.

My new dream goes like this: In the middle of the desert, my father takes off his boots and shakes out pebbles, dirt, dead leaves. Lizards crawl around, looking for shade under rocks and short shrubs. When he untwists the top of the canteen, he finds nothing inside.

You drank all the water, he says.

Yes, I say, I was thirsty.

That's all we had left, he says. We won't be able to survive.

A quarter mile away stands a giant cactus plant.

I'll race you for the water in the cactus, I say.

He unstraps the canteen from his belt, takes the backpack off his shoulders, and gives both the canteen and the backpack to me. After stretching his legs by touching his toes and doing deep knee bends, he builds up sand to serve as a starting block and crouches down in a sprinter's position. With his feet buried in the sand, his shoulders hunched over and shaking, and his head pointed straight ahead as if he's a bird dog, he rocks until he's set. He's serious.

Who's going to start us? I ask.

Runners, he says, spitting into the dirt, take your marks.

Are you sure—

Get set.

I'd hate for you—

Go, he says. He gets off to such a good start that I think maybe he's jumped the gun. I chase after him, calling out that in order to be absolutely fair to both parties involved we should at least think about starting over again, but he ignores me, clenches his fists, and lengthens his stride, kicking up pebbles. Bounding over the desert, avoiding rocks and brush, we approach the cactus plant, which is huge: four stems curve up from the base and one major stem sticks straight up into the air thirty feet like a thick green finger.

I can hear him gasping for breath when I edge up on him, but I have nothing in reserve: my head's bobbing up and down; my neck muscles are straining. He brings his knees up higher, all the way to his chest. He sprints away from me, shouting, racing for the cactus, really hitting his stride, his arms and legs working together smoothly and powerfully.

My knees buckle and I tumble into the dirt headfirst, arms stretched out flat to break my fall. I scrape my hands on rocks. My dad takes the knife out of his pocket, cuts a low stem of the cactus, cups water in his hands, drinks. He wins. He wins again. He always wins—except in the sense that in the end he'll lose, as we all do.

PERMISSIONS ACKNOWLEDGMENTS

Grateful acknowledgment is made to the following for permission to reprint previously published material:

The Immortality Institute: Excerpt from "Nanomedicine" by Robert A. Freitas Jr., J.D., from *The Scientific Conquest of Death: Essays on Infinite Lifespans*, edited by members of The Immortality Institute (Buenos Aires: LibrosEnRed, 2004). Reprinted by permission of The Immortality Institute.

London Review of Books: Excerpt from "Holy Disorders" by Hilary Mantel (*London Review of Books*, March 4, 2004, vol. 26, no. 5, www .lrb.co.uk). Reprinted by permission of *London Review of Books*.

New Directions Publishing Corp. and David Higham Associates: Excerpt from "The Force That Through the Green Fuse Drives the Flower" from *The Poems of Dylan Thomas*, copyright © 1939 by New Directions Publishing Corp. Reprinted by permission of New Directions Publishing Corp. and David Higham Associates.

The Wylie Agency: Excerpt from "The School" from *Sixty Stories* by Donald Barthelme, copyright © 1976 by Donald Barthelme. Reprinted by permission of The Wylie Agency.

DAVID SHIELDS

REALITY HUNGER

Reality Hunger is a manifesto for a burgeoning group of interrelated but unconnected artists who, living in an unbearably artificial world, are breaking ever larger chunks of 'reality' into their work. The questions Shields explores – the bending of form and genre, the lure and blur of the real – play out constantly around us, and *Reality Hunger* is a radical reframing of how we might think about this 'truthiness': about literary licence, quotation, and appropriation in television, film, performance art, rap, and graffiti, in lyric essays, prose poems, and collage novels.

Drawing on myriad sources, Shields takes an audacious stance on issues that are being fought over now and will be fought over far into the future. Converts will see *Reality Hunger* as a call to arms; detractors will view it as an occasion to defend the status quo. It is certain to provoke impassioned debate for years to come.

'I've just finished reading *Reality Hunger* and I'm lit up by it – astonished, intoxicated, ecstatic, overwhelmed' Jonathan Lethem

'A rare and very peculiar thing: a wake-up call that is a pleasure to hear and respond to. A daring combination of montage and essay, it's crammed full of good things' Geoff Dyer

'One of the most provocative books I've ever read' Charles D'Ambrosio

He just wanted a decent book to read ...

Not too much to ask, is it? It was in 1935 when Allen Lane, Managing Director of Bodley Head Publishers, stood on a platform at Exeter railway station looking for something good to read on his journey back to London. His choice was limited to popular magazines and poor-quality paperbacks – the same choice faced every day by the vast majority of readers, few of whom could afford hardbacks. Lane's disappointment and subsequent anger at the range of books generally available led him to found a company – and change the world.

'We believed in the existence in this country of a vast reading public for intelligent books at a low price, and staked everything on it'
Sir Allen Lane, 1902–1970, founder of Penguin Books

The quality paperback had arrived – and not just in bookshops. Lane was adamant that his Penguins should appear in chain stores and tobacconists, and should cost no more than a packet of cigarettes.

Reading habits (and cigarette prices) have changed since 1935, but Penguin still believes in publishing the best books for everybody to enjoy. We still believe that good design costs no more than bad design, and we still believe that quality books published passionately and responsibly make the world a better place.

So wherever you see the little bird – whether it's on a piece of prize-winning literary fiction or a celebrity autobiography, political tour de force or historical masterpiece, a serial-killer thriller, reference book, world classic or a piece of pure escapism – you can bet that it represents the very best that the genre has to offer.

Whatever you like to read – trust Penguin.